Erasing
Institutional
Bias

Erasing Institutional Bias

How to Create Systemic Change for Organizational Inclusion

Tiffany Jana
and
Ashley Diaz Mejias

Berrett–Koehler Publishers, Inc.
a BK Business book

Berrett-Koehler Publishers, Inc.
1333 Broadway, Suite 1000
Oakland, CA 94612-1921
Tel: (510) 817-2277
Fax: (510) 817-2278
www.bkconnection.com

ORDERING INFORMATION

Quantity sales. Special discounts are available on quantity purchases by corporations, associations, and others. For details, contact the "Special Sales Department" at the Berrett-Koehler address above.

Individual sales. Berrett-Koehler publications are available through most bookstores. They can also be ordered directly from Berrett-Koehler: Tel: (800) 929-2929; Fax: (802) 864-7626; www.bkconnection.com.

Orders for college textbook/course adoption use. Please contact Berrett-Koehler: Tel: (800) 929-2929; Fax: (802) 864-7626.

Distributed to the U.S. trade and internationally by Penguin Random House Publisher Services.

Berrett-Koehler and the BK logo are registered trademarks of Berrett-Koehler Publishers, Inc.

Printed in Canada

Berrett-Koehler books are printed on long-lasting acid-free paper. When it is available, we choose paper that has been manufactured by environmentally responsible processes. These may include using trees grown in sustainable forests, incorporating recycled paper, minimizing chlorine in bleaching, or recycling the energy produced at the paper mill.

Library of Congress Cataloging-in-Publication Data
Names: Jana, Tiffany, author. | Diaz Mejias, Ashley, author.
Title: Erasing institutional bias : how to create systemic change for organizational inclusion / Tiffany Jana, Ashley Diaz Mejias ; foreword by Jay Coen Gilbert.
Description: First Edition. | Oakland : Berrett-Koehler Publishers, 2018.
Identifiers: LCCN 2018030051 | ISBN 9781523097579 (paperback)
Subjects: LCSH: Discrimination in employment. | Personnel management. |
  Industrial relations. | BISAC: BUSINESS & ECONOMICS / Workplace Culture. |
  BUSINESS & ECONOMICS / Human Resources & Personnel Management. | SOCIAL
  SCIENCE / Discrimination & Race Relations.
Classification: LCC HD4903 .J36 2018 | DDC 658.3008--dc23
LC record available at https://lccn.loc.gov/2018030051First Edition

23 22 21 20 19 18   10 9 8 7 6 5 4 3 2 1

Interior design and production: Dovetail Publishing Services
Cover designer: Dan Tesser / Studio Carnelian

Dedications

Tiffany Jana
To my eldest daughter, Naomi Vickers, an inspiration to all around her.

Ashley Diaz Mejias
For my daughters Belen, Maisy, and Yves.
With a soul-dwelling awe at the light that lives in each of you.

Contents

Foreword

by Jay Coen Gilbert, cofounder, B Lab,
serving the B Corporation movement

Only 43 percent of B Lab's staff who are people of color feel they can bring their whole selves to work, compared to 96 percent of their white coworkers.

The words hit me like a punch to the gut. As a person who cares deeply about equity, I have spent considerable time and resources and dedicated my professional and civic life for the last decade to building a more equitable society and a more inclusive economy, so reading this statistic from a recent staff survey devastated me.

It also shouldn't have surprised me.

B Lab, the organization I cofounded in 2006, is the nonprofit behind the global B Corporation movement. B Corporations redefine success in business—they compete to be best *for* the world and meet the most rigorous standards of social and environmental performance, public transparency, and legal accountability to balance profit and purpose. There are roughly 2,500 Certified B Corporations in more than 150 industries and 50 countries all dedicated to a single unifying goal—using the power of business to create an inclusive economy that works for everyone. B Corps have been called one of the "20 Moments That Mattered" over the last 20 years by *Fast Company*, and one of the "Business Trends to Master" by *Fortune*. B Corps have been lauded by a Nobel Prize–winning economist, a former US president, former US secretaries of labor and state, and dozens of governors across the political spectrum who are inspired by B Corporations' new model of inclusive corporate governance that ensures consideration of all stakeholders—not just shareholders—when making decisions. B Lab has been honored as a recipient of the Skoll Award for Social Entrepreneurship and of the McNulty Prize at the Aspen Institute. And yet, only 43 percent of B Lab's staff who are people of color feel they can bring their whole selves to work, compared to 96 percent of their white coworkers.

Houston, we have a problem.

B Lab, an organization of roughly 65 people, is 68 percent white—whiter than the US population, which according to the 2016 estimates by the US Census Bureau is 61 percent white, non-Hispanic white. That wasn't what surprised me. What surprised me was that the staff survey suggested that our culture was more like 98 percent white. More specifically, white middle-to-upper-class culture. I learned that there were things I never noticed that were negatively impacting our team's experience at work. For example, our primary office location is in a largely white affluent suburb and that has created an unwelcoming environment for some team members. Other issues seemed to be about class and culture as well as the interconnected issue of race: our expense reimbursement policy assumes our colleagues have credit cards (we don't offer corporate cards) and is ignorant to the fact that some who do might be put in a tough spot if we reimbursed them after they needed to pay their monthly bill (more burdensome because research that suggests credit terms are often worse for people of color than for whites); personal shares at our weekly staff meeting, intended to build connection and community, often featured photos from a team member's amazing travel experience or beautiful wedding, which for some had a "must be nice for you" dissonant ring; general office chatter—whether in the kitchen, on Slack, or during GoToMeetings—reflected the life experiences, interests, and digital feeds of our team, and since that team was largely white and privileged, or then just being around the office was a daily reminder of "otherness" and an obstacle for some to bring their whole selves to work every day. Compounding these issues, B Lab had almost no people of color in leadership, creating a lack of role models for career development and compounding a sense of isolation. Perhaps that is why people of color at B Lab were more likely to experience social interactions at work as "poor or fair" vs. "good or great."

One of the things we learn in Dr. Jana's and Diaz Mejias' book *Erasing Institutional Bias* is to be data-driven. The quantitative and qualitative results of our staff survey were a cold-shower reminder for me to look at the data and not to trust blindly in my own personal experience, which may be quite different from the experience of others, including others whom I care about and think I know well. Despite the pain I felt learning this information, I would have been far more devastated had I and our management team remained oblivious any longer. Data—and the deeper understanding it can offer—creates opportunities. This data gave us the information we needed to begin to improve the experiences, and hopefully the success and longevity, of people of color at B Lab. While we have a long way to go, changes to these policies, to our everyday business practices, and to our leadership team are underway. These changes will make us a stronger team that makes better decisions and builds a stronger, more inclusive global movement of people using business as a force for good.

In this book, Dr. Jana and Diaz Mejias take us through the many and intersecting types of bias, including occupational, gender, racial, hiring/advancement, customer, and retribution, showing us the nuances of these biases and ways they play out in our lives and in our workplaces. I can say from the vantage point of B Lab and the B Corp community that even with the best of intentions, each of these biases can manifest in a very real and present way. One that has felt most pressing for B Lab, and for me personally, has been bias in hiring and advancement.

If a non-inclusive culture and bias is more likely to persist in a homogeneous culture, then a necessary step in building an inclusive culture and eradicating institutional bias ought to be building a more heterogeneous culture. That means diversifying the team—at all levels—to ensure more heterogeneous perspectives and experiences can show up in the everyday interactions that create culture, and can add value to solving problems and seizing opportunities that create great organizations.

In my experience, that is often easier said than done.

We all tend to have networks that resemble ourselves. For example, according to research by Public Religion Research Institute (PRRI), 75 percent of white people do not have a significant relationship with a person or family of color. Another example, holding Boys Night Out and Girls Night Out events are fun and can be important safe spaces, but they can reinforce monogender personal networks. From my experience, building heterogeneous teams and cultures requires intention and commitment.

For those who lack intention or commitment, and for whom erasing bias isn't self-sufficient motivation, there is plenty of research that makes a compelling business case for building diverse and inclusive teams and culture. As the report "The Competitive Advantage of Racial Equity" from the consulting firm FSG states, "Research shows that more diverse teams are better able to solve problems and that companies with more diverse workforces have higher revenues, more customers, and greater market shares." As someone who came to B Lab after 13 years building a basketball footwear and apparel company called AND1, I often default to sports metaphors. For those with a similar bent, from a purely competitive point of view, your team will beat my team if my team only uses half of its available players.

At B Lab, our biggest obstacle has not been intention or commitment, it has been time. Like many organizations, for-profit or nonprofit, the team at B Lab is running hard all the time. People put in long days, often nights and some weekends, to advance what we feel is important work. For every team member, there is always way more to do in a day, a week, a month, than can be done. As my partner likes to say, we will always be "over-opportunitied and under-resourced."

In an environment like this, every person's understandable reflex when filling open positions is to fill them fast. Help is on the way! Get someone talented and aligned on board ASAP. Faster if possible. As a result, we too often value a speedy hiring decision over a strategic hiring decision. That often means we have filled full time positions with interns—aka easily accessible, known quantities who have demonstrated they can do the work and are a good cultural fit. And they can start tomorrow. At one point, roughly one-third of all B Lab staff were former interns. As in many organizations, interns often come from our personal networks—the schools we attended, a neighbor or colleague's child, or just local talent with the life experience that has taught them that the world is theirs if they work hard and self-advocate. For an organization like B Lab, with primary offices located in an affluent suburb of Philadelphia, cofounded by three white people, this means our interns have looked almost entirely like us. And, since we have often promoted from within, this desired internal upward mobility—great for career development—can have the unintended effect of elevating a homogeneous culture, especially when we backfill with interns who reflect the existing team, their implicit biases, and our collective prioritization of speed over strategy.

Dr. Jana and Diaz Mejias' book asks us to reflect on how each of us individually may contribute to creating or perpetuating institutional bias in our organizations. As I reflected, I realized I have personally exacerbated the difficulties of building an inclusive and diverse team by—likely among other things—creating and perpetuating a culture that prioritizes speed over strategy. Not only do I work fast and long hours, thus creating expectations of the same, but I am an idea-generating machine that sees opportunity everywhere and creates energy to turn safe-to-try ideas into dangerous-to-implement initiatives that overburden an already overstretched team. My pace, passion, ability to make connections and see opportunities, when coupled with a lack of adequate self-restraint, has too often pushed us to hire faster, not smarter, as people understandably grasp for the nearest life preserver to carry them through the next set of waves. This is at least one way I need to change my behavior to support the team in achieving our shared objective of building an inclusive, diverse, and best-in-class organization. Hiring outside of our existing personal and professional networks will require a sustained effort to identify partners, to explore areas of alignment, and to build trust. That will take time, and I need to change my behavior to create the space to make that possible.

A similar dynamic exists for building an inclusive, diverse B Corp community worthy of being called leaders.

A community of business leaders cofounded by three white guys tends to beget more white guys. When building a community of business leaders (and society has created a situation in which most business leaders are white men), then it's likely that without explicit intention, commitment, time, and money focused on building a heterogeneous community, we are destined to get what we got—a largely white male community.

There are other factors at work, too, that have made progress more difficult. Despite intention to diversify our community, many team members are limited in their knowledge of—let alone relationship with—other professional networks serving underrepresented communities. Some may also feel reticent to lean in to build relationships with these networks, feeling unequipped, or even perhaps a little intimidated, to engage with, for example, communities of color about our work and how it may or may not resonate with their personal or business objectives.

As the staff survey illustrated, we have also been too slow to recognize the importance of inclusion in addition to the value of diversity. It is only recently, thanks to the thoughtfulness and advocacy of B Lab's Equity, Diversity, and Inclusion Committee, that we have spent time and resources creating more inclusive event design and more inclusive language and imagery in our marketing and communications. We have only just begun to think through the implications of the fact that women and entrepreneurs of color may have different needs and priorities that ought to shape the services and products we offer, and that drive their particular value proposition for deciding whether it is worth the time, effort, and money to join the B Corp community. For example: women- and people of color–led businesses have a much harder time raising capital; they have more limited social networks of privilege, power, and resources; they are burdened with society-imposed biases that further limit their opportunities, which could be exacerbated if they are also seen by the gatekeepers to powerful business and investor networks as leading "less serious do-good" businesses. All of these truths exist and make the reality of being a women- or person of color–led business different than being a white- or especially a white male–led business. With this understanding, we need to shape our offerings accordingly, and are beginning to do so.

Despite the many challenges, while the efforts of B Lab and the B Corp community to lead by example have been slow and flawed, they have been real.

We all have implicit bias and, as a result, so do our communities and our institutions. The B Corp community reflects the business community at large, and the business community reflects society. Hundreds of years of inequity have created a society in which only 3 percent of US businesses with employees are owned by people of color and only 4 percent are owned by women. While 29 percent of US businesses are owned by people of color, and 37 percent are owned by women, approximately 90 percent of businesses owned by people of color and by women are solopreneurs with no employees. Six percent of US B Corps with employees are led by people of color and 23 percent by women. In a glass-half-full world, regarding people of color– and women-led businesses with employees, the B Corp community is two times (for people of color) and nearly six times (for women) as diverse as the US business community. In a glass-half-empty world, 6 percent and 23 percent are still unacceptably low, robbing our community and our society of the value that would be created for all of us by a more diverse community of leaders.

Institutional bias goes beyond the walls of any single institution. The further bias gets from individual human bias, the harder it can be to see if we don't know where or how to look. Take the implicit bias of the legal structure of the corporation itself. The legal principle of shareholder primacy states that corporations are obligated to maximize value for shareholders. This creates an economic system full of well-intentioned people who are legally obligated to make decisions that benefit only, or at least overwhelmingly, those with the financial capital to own shares. And who owns those shares is illuminating. Only about 10 percent of Americans own nearly 85 percent of the shares of all the companies traded in the stock market; nearly 50 percent of Americans do not own a single share of a single company. The path to ownership, and thus to influence, over corporate behavior is even more difficult for people of color. Given hundreds of years of slavery, racial terror, and discrimination, black Americans have very little financial capital compared to their white fellow citizens (for example, black families have $0.05 cents of wealth for every $1.00 dollar of wealth owned by white families; that figure is $0.06 cents for Latino families), giving them less opportunity to have a say in governing the behavior of corporations. B Corporations address this systemic institutional bias by voluntarily holding themselves to a higher standard of legal accountability which requires B Corps to consider the impact of their decisions on all of their stakeholders—their workers, their communities, the environment—and not just their shareholders.

B Corps not only institutionalize inclusive corporate governance, but also take action to increase their inclusive business practices. Today, hundreds of B Corps of all sizes in dozens of industries are participating in B Lab's Inclusive Economy Challenge, which invites companies to set and meet three goals in order to use their business as a means of advancing equity and inclusion. The list of potential goals goes well beyond human resources–focused diversity training to use the power of individual businesses to address systemic marginalization and lack of opportunity including issues such as living wage, gender pay equity, inclusive supply chains, and distributed ownership.

I believe more in karma than coincidence, so it was not surprising to me that I received Dr. Jana and Diaz Mejias' manuscript not long after our management team was presented with the data on the inclusiveness and diversity of our organization and our community. Thirsty for insights and resources, I began to devour the book, realizing quickly that this text laid the groundwork for me not only to understand how my perception of staff experience could deviate so far from reality, but also how I could move from feeling devastated to motivated. Dr. Jana and Diaz Mejias offer practical, actionable ideas that can transform problems into solutions.

One of the most powerful effects the book had on me was affirming the power in owning and naming the challenges we experience in turning our intentions into actions and our actions into results. This is especially true for white-led businesses and business communities from which we too often hear either a deafening silence on these issues or which have the mistaken perception that institutional bias is a problem for "others," not "us," a perception that prevents organizations and society from reaching their full potential. As Dr. Jana says, "we are all are part of the problem if we are participating in systems without questioning and leveraging our influence." As I prepared myself to write this foreword, I felt an eerily familiar feeling, a mixture of excitement and anxiety. The feeling just before taking a big risk, in this case, turning a private belief into a public commitment and thereby creating accountability for leveraging the kind of transparency that creates vulnerability and the potential for transformation.

I met Dr. Jana in 2013 when she came to B Lab and then to our staff retreat to lead our team through our first inclusion, diversity, and equity training. Her company, TMI Consulting, which specializes in helping companies unlock innovation through inclusion, had become a Certified B Corporation the year before. From the frameworks she shared, the exercises she led us through, and the conversations she helped us have, I knew her work would dramatically change my business. Our team then invited Dr. Jana to share her insights and to deliver a challenge to the B Corp community as a keynote speaker of our first public B Inspired event in 2015. She delivered, and since then Dr. Jana has been a much sought out thought partner to B Lab and to many in our community working on these issues. Although we have a long way to go at B Lab and in the B Corp community to live up to our highest aspirations, we have made huge progress since starting our journey, in large part thanks to our invaluable partnership with Dr. Jana. I am grateful that each of you and your organizations have the opportunity to be transformed by Dr. Jana's work. Dr. Jana and Diaz Mejias' book has tools to help us move beyond the more common, but less effective, frame of bias identification to instead sketch a clear, actionable roadmap to behavior and systems change. Once we understand bias and systemic oppression, what next? Dr. Jana and Diaz Mejias answer this crucial question for us.

At this moment in history, we cannot afford to continue ignoring the inequities disproportionately affecting marginalized, vulnerable, and historically underrepresented communities. We can, and must, work individually, organizationally, and collectively as part of a deliberate, coordinated movement to dismantle the systems built by bias and create a new normal—a purpose-driven inclusive economy that works for everyone.

Read this book. Let it inspire you to move from hopeful intention to skillful action.

Introduction

How Ordinary People Can Identify and Eliminate Institutional Bias

Erasing Institutional Bias: How to Create Systemic Change for Organizational Inclusion is the follow up to *Overcoming Bias: Building Authentic Relationships Across Differences*. The focus of the first book was on interpersonal bias and how individuals could address their own hidden perspectives. *Erasing Institutional Bias (EIB)* was written because bias also operates at a systems level as systems are created by humans.

Interpersonal sexism might lead a person to make an inadvertently sexist assumption about a person based on gender. For example, when a man and a woman from the same company walk into a business meeting and people assume the man holds the higher position because of his gender. Things like this happen all the time, and that was the focus of *Overcoming Bias*.

When bias operates at the systems, or institutional level, it acts as a social force and instead of impacting people one by one, it affects many people. If a gender bias is disrupting the balance of an organization at the systems level, it can show up in a number of overt and subtle ways including:

1. A disproportionately high number of people who identify as male dominating leadership positions in a company relative to the number of people who identify as females in the organization, community, or number of female applicants.

2. Assuming that the women in the office will wash the dishes or bring the baked goods.
3. Negative feedback toward men who don't "man up" and desire dominant, leadership roles in the workplace.
4. Negative feedback toward women who do "man up" by exhibiting confidence and assertiveness.
5. Interpersonal sexism that is allowed to persist within an organization (for example, comments that reduce women or men to sexual objects).

This is a short sample of an infinite number of large and small ways systemic bias can infect an organizational culture. Even language carries implicit bias, and the authors acknowledge the complexity of gender identity in particular. While you may see the linguistic gender binary used throughout the book, we invite all people to see themselves reflected within our conceptual framework. The other institutional biases we will discuss in this book in addition to gender bias include:

Racial Bias   An implicit preference of one race over another.

Occupational Bias   An implicit bias that assigns fixed human or demographic attributes to a particular job or career.

Hiring/Advancement Bias   Any implicit preference that creates hiring and advancement opportunities that privilege one group over another.

Customer Bias   Any *interpersonal* bias that supports valuing some customers over others. (For example, assuming that foreign people aren't good potential customers/clients/donors because they don't speak your language or have enough money.)

Retribution Bias   An implicit assumption that exacting retribution is of greater consequence than preserving or maintaining a relationship.[1]

All humans have bias, and as a result, so do the institutions we build. This is an increasingly relevant topic as evidenced by increased media coverage about bias across various industries and sectors, and countries—from Hollywood to Wall Street and Saudi Arabia to Haiti, people from different backgrounds are unable to access equitable opportunities and experiences.

This book will help you identify and address the systemic and institutional bias that results from the pernicious and often unconscious biases to which we are all vulnerable. We hope to help you see how we are all contributing to the marginalization of people in our communities and around the world through both our actions and inaction. We aspire to offer individuals and institutions practical, actionable solutions to large scale, systemic inequities.

Systemic Marginalization Is a Global Human Phenomenon

It's one thing for people to be overly biased and choose to build discriminatory systems. We have seen this phenomenon with the misguided laws and policies of nations designed to intimidate, marginalize, and limit access and opportunity for specific groups of people. Redlining and Jim Crow in the United States, Apartheid in South Africa, and Pakistan's Hudood Ordinances are a few examples. Conscious and unconscious biases, like racial and gender bias, can lead to the creation of workplaces that largely promote specific races and genders. Hiring bias can lead to homogeneous workplaces comprised of people with similar educational experiences and other similar characteristics. Occupational bias can lead to the systematic marginalization of people based on their job function or occupational status. Nurses are notoriously sidelined and treated as second-class employees compared to doctors. Stay-at-home parents are some of the hardest working people on the planet, yet their careers as homemakers are often marginalized and penalized when those homemaking years appear as gaps from traditional employment on resumes. These biases and many others are adversely affecting workplaces, neighborhoods, and nations every single day.

We are all are part of the problem if we are participating in systems without questioning and leveraging our influence. This book was written to help you understand what systemic bias is, how it is perpetuated, and how you can disrupt its mechanisms and erode its power. We hope to enlist your help in tearing down the walls that divide us.

From Overcoming Bias to Erasing Institutional Bias

Many readers who sought out *Overcoming Bias* asked us to write this book. People who are concerned with the way inequity leads to disparate experiences and outcomes will want to read this book. People who don't want to wait for someone else to instigate change should read this book. The change makers and the people inspired to take control and make a difference by leveraging their own privilege should read this book. This book is also for employees and students of institutions who wish to create less biased systems. It is also for leaders who wish to change their organizations.

Overcoming Bias helped individuals overcome their interpersonal bias. *Erasing Institutional Bias* will help you tackle structural bias regardless of your positional power. One of the problems with systemic bias is that erasing it seems an insurmountable task from the vantage point of a single individual. This book will help you recognize that each of us has the power to affect systemic bias through deliberate, coordinated effort.

As a diversity and inclusion practitioner, Tiffany Jana has worked with countless clients who recognize that bias may be operating at the systems level within their organizations. The problem is that the bias is so embedded that they usually don't know how to mitigate it. Then there are the clients who don't recognize that bias is at play but know that something is amiss. If one person within an institutional system reads this book, they will have sufficient data to articulate the challenges clearly and offer workable solutions.

When bias is addressed at the organizational level, a more diverse group of people makes the organization more successful. When more people thrive within an organization, the mission and vision can be realized with greater efficiency and focus. As organizations realize their missions, society will be impacted. For-profit companies will be more profitable and nonprofits will improve conditions and outcomes for people around the world.

Structural bias is not created overnight. The bias that permeates institutions, systems, and economies is carefully crafted over long periods of time. Sometimes the destructive, exclusive nature of institutional bias is deliberately designed. Often the unconscious bias of individuals and groups makes its way into organized systems and wreaks havoc regardless of its creator's intentions. The good news is that most of what has been done can be undone. That is not to say undoing things doesn't necessarily come at great cost, but it can be done with careful thought and deliberate action. Erasing institutional bias is possible.

Erasing institutional bias requires a series of steps. These steps are by no means the only way to reduce or eliminate systemic bias. They are one set of interventions that, when enacted, can be effective. First, you have to look at what you are bringing into the situation. All work on bias should begin with introspection. Further steps include actions you can take to connect with others and affect systemic changes.

Chapter 1 examines the first step: identifying what type of systemic bias is present. Chapter 2 includes discussion on how to evaluate your role in perpetuating institutional bias and how to break it down instead. Breaking down systemic bias will require cultivating allies, as described in chapter 2. Chapters 3–9 will include the detailed process for eradicating institutional bias once you've clarified your old and new roles and cultivated allies. You cannot do it entirely alone, but it can *start* with you.

We developed two primary frameworks for you to reference as you erase institutional bias. The first includes the work you must do before examining institutional bias challenges. The second is the actual work of addressing bias within larger systems. These frameworks are overviews of steps that will be expanded in detail throughout the remainder of the book.

FRAMEWORK 1

Personal EIB Change Framework

Before embarking on the hard work of erasing institutional bias, you will need to:

1. Evaluate your (old) role in perpetuating systemic bias.

2. Define your (new) role in breaking down systemic bias.

3. Cultivate allies.

4. Create a movement.

These four preliminary steps will be explained in detail in chapter 2. The remaining chapters expand on the following six steps for erasing institutional bias:

FRAMEWORK 2

Institutional EIB Change Framework

1. Set a clear intention.

2. Lead with data.

3. Diagnose accurately.

4. Deconstruct: eliminate subjective processes.

5. Reconstruct with objectivity.

6. Build in accountability and ongoing measurement.

We believe that by doing the preliminary personal EIB work and implementing the six steps in the Institutional EIB Change Framework, determined individuals can work in concert with like-minded collaborators to instigate sustainable institutional change.

Chapter One

Understanding the Problem

Institutional or systemic bias is the phenomenon that exists when some groups maintain advantage over others within the context of a particular structure. Institutional bias is the result of interpersonal bias that has been institutionalized, or embedded within systems. Each of the biases enumerated in this book can operate at the interpersonal level *and* the institutional level. The examples of bias in this book are operating at the institutional level unless otherwise stated. The institutional biases that we will expand upon in this book include in the following order:

Occupational Bias   An implicit bias that assigns fixed human or demographic attributes to a particular job or career.

Gender Bias   An implicit bias that assigns fixed attributes by gender and/or privileges one gender over another.

Racial Bias   An implicit preference of one race over another.

Hiring/Advancement Bias   Any implicit preference that creates hiring and advancement opportunities that privilege one group over another.

Customer Bias   Any interpersonal bias that supports valuing some customers over others. (For example, assuming that foreign people aren't good potential customers/clients/donors because they don't speak your language or have enough money.)

Retribution Bias   An implicit assumption that exacting retribution is of greater consequence than preserving or maintaining a relationship.

Interpersonal bias includes the human preferences and assumptions we have for, against, and about each other. Interpersonal biases include racism, sexism, homophobia, xenophobia, ageism, the tendency to like or dislike people based on variables like weight, political affiliation, leadership status, intelligence, education, religion, socioeconomic class, or anything that defines people. Sometimes the biases are based on things people cannot change, like race, or things they can, like politics. Either way, interpersonal bias is what divides us and compromises our ability to build healthy, diverse relationships with all kinds of people. If you think of interpersonal bias as a single germ—a toxic little antagonist that can destroy healthy cells—then institutional bias is an infection, an outbreak of a germ at scale that can sicken or obliterate an entire system.

When one group is allowed to prosper over others for extended periods of time, systemic bias is usually at play. Are we attempting to create systems in which all people can thrive? Do we care whether people have equal opportunities to excel and advance based on individual merit? Are we more concerned with advancing people who think like us? Are we creating opportunities for people who went to our schools, with whom we share social interactions and interests? What kind of world and what kind of workplaces are we cultivating? The world arguably consists of systems that have already been optimized to yield the results we see today. These may be results that work for some, but there are a great many people who see imbalance and injustice in the systems we have today.

This book is designed to raise awareness about the imbalance in the collective consciousness and help us hold ourselves accountable for creating a world that works for everyone. Many of our readers may be in more formalized organizational settings such as corporate workplaces or civic organizations. This means that many of you will have some form of organizational power that you can access, whether you are in a small or large organization. Though we are writing with these environments in mind, we are drawing on research and conclusions that have implications for almost all areas of life. In other words, the benefits of creating more equitable organizations translate into the world at large. This is good for everyone!

However, we are writing and drawing on examples of people who are, for the most part, working to instigate change from within organizations. It is important that we acknowledge that many people in the world have been completely marginalized and excluded from the benefits of systemic or organizational power and are looking for ways to organize and work for equity from outside traditional and established organizations. While we believe our insights can support that work, we aren't writing explicitly to those circumstances simply because our scope is limited to the areas of our expertise.

We have become accustomed to cultivating systems that work well for those in power, those with wealth and connections, and those with access to the levers of change within systems. We have mountains of research that prove that diversity and inclusion help create smarter, more effective, more profitable systems. If diversity serves the greater good, whether economic or social, why have we not developed our systems to optimize inclusion?

How do you erase institutional bias?

Institutional bias can be erased if each of us owns our individual responsibility to be part of the solution. How many times have you witnessed something in an organization and known darn well that it was unfair? Maybe you are even self-aware enough already to be able to acknowledge a time in your career when *you* were the person responsible for carrying out an action that was unfair or biased. We propose that each of us starts with ourselves and go through the four steps we shared in the Introduction:

FRAMEWORK 1

Personal EIB Change Framework: Individual Prework

1. Evaluate your (old) role in perpetuating systemic bias.
2. Define your (new) role in breaking down systemic bias.
3. Cultivate allies.
4. Create a movement.

Once you have done that, you can take on the six steps to erasing institutional bias. Each of the following steps will be expanded with examples from people and institutions that have succeeded in moving the needles toward greater organizational inclusion.

FRAMEWORK 2

Organizational EIB Change Framework

1. Set a clear intention.
2. Lead with data.
3. Diagnose accurately.
4. Deconstruct: eliminate subjective processes.
5. Reconstruct with objectivity.
6. Build in accountability and ongoing measurement.

It is important to note that the systems we have operating in our world today are systems of our own design. Maybe not you and me specifically, but human beings set forth to create organizational systems, bias and all, quite deliberately. Of course, the people who designed these systems made them hospitable for themselves and people like them. That statement is not intended to stereotype or pigeonhole any particular group other than those with the power to construct systems. The people in power will look different from nation to nation. They may vary by gender, race, ethnicity, religion, education, beliefs, and so on. What these social architects have in common is power. They share an outsized influence on society, communities, and people who choose (or must function) within those systems.

We are proposing that we work to erase institutional bias because those of us adversely affected by these systems are fed up. And many of us who have outsized power and influence to affect systemic change are equally fed up. This isn't just about David confronting Goliath. More and more, mighty giants are standing up in the face of the selfsame institutional bias they have supported to say enough is enough. They, too, are aware of the problem and, in many cases, are prepared to be part of the solution. The best example we have of this is the B Corp community. B Corps are for-profit companies that choose to include society and the environment as stakeholders to whom they are accountable. Recently, a significant subset of the B Corp community decided to up the ante and participate in the Inclusive Economy Challenge. B Lab says:

> *Launched in 2016, the Inclusive Economy Challenge is a call to action for the B Corp Community to increase our collective positive impact and move toward an inclusive economy. An inclusive economy is one that is equitable and creates opportunity for all people of all backgrounds and experiences to live with dignity, to support themselves and their families, and to help their communities thrive. The B Corp Community's vision of a shared and durable prosperity is not possible without an inclusive economy.*
>
> *The Inclusive Economy Challenge provides accountability, targeted resources, and a structure of*

> *peer learning to help participating companies tackle*
> *complex, sensitive, and urgent issues.*

So, the obvious question is: how are we going to erase institutional bias? We are certain you are thinking, hey, if it were possible, wouldn't institutional bias already be erased? The short answer is no. The authors of this book are optimists with more than a healthy dose of skepticism. The reality of the situation is that the world has not been ready to erase institutional bias and may not be just yet. But we are closer to achieving a critical mass of people who want to see real change and are willing to go to bat to make it happen. This is certainly the case in the United States.

Every so often, significant historical events serve as wake-up calls to communities and nations. Anything from a national election to the public shaming of high-profile leaders and celebrities can reveal evidence of institutional bias in governments, industries, and sectors of economy. Sometimes biased decisions made in the past are carried forward past the point of their utility, or past the point when people begin to value inclusion more than their predecessors. For example, the founding fathers of the United States—an oligarchical, self-serving concentration of power if there ever was one—decided to create the Electoral College to prevent average US citizens from electing a president by popular vote. They were biased against common folk and critical of their collective intelligence, so they created a system that placed ultimate power in the hands of a privileged few individuals with the resources and wherewithal to run for and win congressional seats.

Many people believe that as education has become more accessible and as America has led the world in the most inclusive and comprehensive antidiscrimination laws, class and racial tensions are in conflict with the historical system of voting in the USA. The good news is that now it is not solely the historically marginalized people who see the systemic problems and want them addressed; people who fall into the categories of the historically privileged are finally on board. And a million thanks to those who've been on board for years—we see you, too. The difference is that now we have a groundswell. Now we can do something about institutional bias and we will not be ignored.

Theory of Change: How We Make It Happen

The phrase "Theory of Change" sounds complicated and intimidating, but it's really pretty straightforward—it's a way of creating a road map to a desired result. Here, we're all hoping to create more inclusive organizations, or places where people's gender and gender identities, race, occupations, and so on—all the things that could contribute to mistreatment—are no longer disqualifiers. Our theory of change is that we can:

> *Create sustainable systemic change by leveraging data to create tools that hold institutions accountable.*

In other words, if we leverage data and create tools that hold institutions accountable, we absolutely *can* create sustainable change. Our theory of change is based in the reality that our feelings are not reliable sources of information for instigating fair and equitable change. We believe that we must set aside our personal assumptions and feelings and invite experts to provide data. Credible data can help us initiate meaningful conversations, develop metrics-based tools, and make changes that support human equity—especially in organizations.

If we move through our six-step framework (which we will discuss in depth later in this book) and begin to name the things that have gone unnamed, then we will gain power over institutional bias. This is not to say that it will get everyone on board. But leading with data and creating data-driven tools can help us hold ourselves and our institutions accountable for the systemic changes we aim to create.

There is a certain amount of cognitive dissonance that we experience when we first begin to entertain the notion that an institutional system may not be what it appears to be on the surface. We are taught to believe that all job applications get equal and fair consideration. You may have learned this as a young child when warned by a parent to avoid interactions with the police, or you may have learned this as an adult when you saw friends get mistreated in their industry because of race or gender. "The System" is not fair, and if you've picked up this book, it's likely that you want to find a way to make things better.

But how? Well, we can't just trust our instincts. It's important to note that as Americans, we regularly *over-estimate* the diversity of population groups that we're asked to evaluate. A 2013 study released by the Center for American Progress and PolicyLink concluded that Americans vastly overestimate current levels of diversity in the United States, with the average respondent guessing that 49 percent of the nation is minority.[1] The actual figure is closer to 37 percent. The two largest minority groups being Hispanics and Latinas at 18 percent followed by African Americans making up 13 percent of the US population. Sixty-one percent of the people in the United States identify as white, non-Hispanic, or Latino.

People's tendency to overestimate minority populations in the United States leads to disproportionate concern about who is taking over jobs, committing crimes, and generally taking over the US population as some people have come to know it. Those assumptions affect people's attitudes and opinions about level-setting programs like Affirmative Action and Welfare. Would people feel differently about social programs that affect marginalized communities if they had data that indicated that more nonminority people actually benefit from government funded programs than minorities? We don't know. But we do know that the conversations would be more productive if we could all start with factual data.

Given the enormity and power of systemic bias in the United States, change can seem virtually impossible. We believe, though, that change actually is possible. Systems were built biased by humans and systems can be dismantled and made just by humans. In order to do this, though, we must begin in our own spheres of influence and be willing to lay down our own personal agendas in favor of what is best for the collective.

Stereotype Threat

Erasing institutional bias isn't just about making your workplace "fair" or maximizing your bottom line, but you probably already guessed that. Erasing institutional bias can actually change the way people—individual people—see themselves in your work-place and in the world and, thus, can actually inspire people to live with more confidence.

Many folks these days are aware enough to avoid using direct stereotypes when dealing with those who are different from them. What's frightening, however, is that those stereotypes have power even when they aren't directly being used, so a stereotype about a person can cause damage even when it isn't being invoked. This kind of destruction is far more insidious and has proven to be far more confusing and catastrophic in studies of minority performance on tests, in job interviews, and in other settings.

This type of subconscious stereotype awareness is called a stereotype threat and is commonly defined as the expectation that one will be judged on the basis of social identity group membership rather than actual performance and potential.[2]

Stereotype threats, which operate at an intuitive level, create crippling anxiety, stress, and fear.

Experiments have demonstrated that when people feel less anxiety and when they feel comfortable, they are judged by conversation partners and observers to be wittier and more intelligent. Stereotype threats, then, invoke negative stereotypes about a group of people to increase anxiety and fear in performance-based settings, many times working like a self-fulfilling prophecy. When people are asked to perform a task and they are worried that their behavior or performance may likely conform to stereotypes about their race, gender, and sexuality, their attention "splits," so to speak.

If you want to understand this more, just think of a time when you felt comfortable with someone and you thought to yourself, "Man, I am really funny!" or "I sound pretty smart!" Or, maybe you can think of a time when the reverse has been true—you've been introduced to someone at a party and mid-conversation you've thought to yourself, "I feel so dumb—I cannot think of a single thing to say to this person." Odds are, you aren't making it up!

The stress of worrying about whatever stereotype they are primed to be concerned with diminishes their ability to actually complete the task they are asked to complete. Psychologists Claude Steele and Joshua Aronson have documented the phenomenon and found that, for example, members of groups found to be academically inferior—such as African Americans and Latinos enrolled in college, or female students in STEM courses—perform significantly worse on tests when they are reminded beforehand of their race or gender.

Why is this important? Well, for starters, it's not just a problem we can think our way out of! In a 2015 study out of Indiana University, researchers studying the impact of stereotype threats on women discovered that not only were stereotype threats found at work, but they also discovered that both men and women surveyed significantly underestimated the impact of these stereo-type threats against women. Prior to completing the tasks, both men and women reported the belief that performing the studied tasks under negative stereotypes about women would be a "moti-vating challenge" and predicted overwhelmingly that the women would "overcome these roadblocks." However, the results of the study confirmed that the women studied reported high levels of anxiety and they did not report high levels of motivation.

In other words, this data confirmed that there was a signifi-cant disconnect between expectations and reality—the vast majority of participants in the study thought that women would know better and could just power through negative stereotypes about themselves. The data, however, showed that these stereo-types have more power than we think. This reality is a significant one that has implications for schools and workplaces. We may just believe that women and minorities in our workplaces should have the willpower and positive mindset to perform a particular way, but research—data—has shown time and time again that ste-reotypes are much more powerful than we think.

Using data and our six-step process can actually improve overall performance and maximize employee potential but, more importantly, it can address the nebulous cloud of anxiety that may be holding back some of your best people. In other words, addressing institutional bias can actually make you and your employees feel better by addressing these stereotype threats. In the next chapters, we will review specific types of institutional bias and begin to define how you can prepare yourself for the challenge of erasing it.

Chapter Two

The first thing you need to do is start with yourself. If you are not the CEO, then you will need support to get people on board and affect change. As an individual, you will need to take the following four steps before you can effectively erase institutional bias. These steps are important if you want the changes to be sustainable and persist beyond your tenure.

EXERCISE 1

Preliminary Work

Step 1. Evaluate your (old) role in perpetuating systemic bias.

Step 2. Define your (new) role in breaking down systemic bias.

Step 3. Cultivate allies.

Step 4. Create a movement.

Now let's break down each of these steps to help you understand how to prepare for the challenging task of erasing institutional bias.

Step 1: Evaluate Your (Old) Role in Perpetuating Systemic Bias

This step is important because all of the work that deals with interpersonal strengths requires a healthy dose of self-awareness. It is difficult to be a credible ally and changemaker when you are actively perpetuating the problems you aim to correct. So, when you identify systemic bias at play, it is critical that you do the hard work of understanding the type of bias, its ramifications, and your role in perpetuating it. Ask yourself the following reflection questions:

EXERCISE 2

Perpetuating Bias Reflection Questions

1. What specific bias is at issue?
2. How is this bias affecting me?
3. How am I benefitting from this bias?
4. How am I hurt or limited by this bias?
5. How is this bias affecting my colleagues and this organization's stakeholders?
6. How might this bias benefit specific demographics?
7. Which groups are hurt or limited by this bias?
8. How will erasing this bias help the aforementioned groups?
9. Who might feel threatened by an attempt to erase this bias?

Once you have reviewed your answers, take time to reflect on the implications of this exercise. The questions about who is adversely affected by the bias help you understand why erasing it is important. The questions about who gains from the persistence of the bias and who may feel threatened by its eradication point toward the objections you may have to overcome and from whom they might arise.

Getting jazzed up about helping people who are suffering from the adverse effects of bias is arguably the easy part. Anyone with half a heart will see why it's important and want to be part of the solution. Realizing that your greatest obstacle to instigating change may be the most powerful people and groups in the organization is a bit less motivating. And this is why we will help you understand how to build a coalition. You will need a groundswell of support to make it happen. The good news is that effective changemakers are not as uncommon as you might think. They are often scattered throughout an organization with varying degrees of access to power. They, too, are in need of supporters and allies to make the case for inclusion and, most importantly, a clear path to implementation.

Step 2: Define Your (New) Role in Breaking Down Systemic Bias

Now that you have evaluated your past role in perpetuating systemic bias, it's time to define your new role in erasing it. We have to take a moment to remind you to give yourself and others grace as you embark on this journey. Institutional bias can be really ugly business. Once you begin to see its effects and examine it closely, it is very hard to "unsee" it. It is also hard to avoid becoming angry, bitter, and jaded about the whole phenomenon. It is, however, very important not to lose sight of the goal. Your purpose in this endeavor is to improve opportunities for people. You need to stay strong, maintain focus, and remain as optimistic as possible.

At this point, you need to compare your old role to the goals you have for breaking down systemic bias. In some cases, you will need to take inverse action from those actions that were counterproductive. In other cases, you will need to define new actions where you were formerly merely a passive bystander. Ask yourself the following reflection questions as you consider your new role:

EXERCISE 3

Role Definition Reflection Questions

1. What is the contribution you want to make as it relates to the specific institutional bias you've identified?
2. What power/leverage/influence do you have within the affected institution?

3. How does your current professional role interact with the institutional bias you've targeted for erasure?

4. How committed are you to staying the course during the bias erasure journey?

5. What are you willing to sacrifice to ensure the success of this endeavor?

6. Are you willing to personally champion this cause?

7. What credibility do you have or can you establish to authentically represent this cause?

Your responses to these reflection questions will help you organize your thoughts and galvanize your commitment to erasing institutional bias. Remember that it is a journey and will therefore require persistence, resilience, and patience. Define a reasonable role for yourself, and we say "reasonable" because if your expectations of yourself are too high it can derail your efforts. You need to be aspirational while still being realistic. Unless you happen to be the CEO or the chairwoman of the board of directors, if you decide that you will personally make all the necessary changes without the support of anyone else, it is likely an unreasonable ambition.

We do not wish to deter anyone, but the more plausible your contribution, the more likely you are to succeed. You can always expand your role as you gain traction; but having to reduce your efforts can be very disheartening. We want to avoid anything that takes the joy out of this process. You are quite possibly saving the world—with our help. One organization at a time, we can erase systemic bias and create a more equitable world for everyone in it. But we need to take baby steps along the way.

Step 3: Cultivate Allies

This step is arguably the single most important step you will take in preparation for erasing institutional bias. Cultivating allies is critical precisely because we cannot affect a substantial, sustainable change at the systems level of an institution without a cohort of like-minded people working toward a shared goal. There is a self-perpetuating phenomenon within systems that allows institutional bias to persist even as players are rotated in and out of the ecosystem. The combination of unwritten rules, organizational norms, and power dynamics often hold imbalances steady even as people realize that bias is at play. With countless individuals either deliberately or inadvertently supporting biased structures, it will take a village to counter that energy.

There is a fantastic video on the internet (https://www.youtube .com/watch?v=GA8z7f7a2Pk) that features a man dancing alone in the middle of a crowded park. The sun is shining and people are going about their picnic and kite flying on the expansive grassy field. The man keeps on dancing alone. Frankly, he looks a little crazy because there's no music audible. He's just happy-dancing alone in the sun in a crowded public place. Eventually, someone walks by and decides that happy-dancing in the park seems like a fun thing to do, so he joins the dancing man. Now there are two people dancing joyfully as if no one was watching. The energy begins to shift as more and more people decide to get on the dance train. The interesting thing is that the first man was alone for an uncomfortably long time for the viewer. The time to get people on board decreased as the number of dancers increased.

We share this story because there is, indeed, power in numbers. One person on a crusade can be easily mistaken for crazy. But if you can get at least one more person to see the value in what you are proposing, you have the makings of a movement. Creating a movement is the final preparatory step. So how do you cultivate allies? Let's revisit the dancing man. The dancing man had a purpose. He was happy-dancing in the park. **His message was clear.** Man. Happy. Dancing. In the sun. **He was not deterred** by the awkward stares, the confused looks, or the mocking giggles. He carried on with his mission—happy-dancing in the park. **He communicated with his entire being that he was committed.** When someone decided to join him, **he made space for them to participate**. He could have told them to buzz off or shut down his energy. Instead he continued the dance. His new ally and subsequent allies followed his lead and maintained that welcoming stance, each keying off the others.

This may seem like a silly metaphor, but the basic tenets are a perfect fit. Ask yourself the following reflection questions before you set a course to cultivate your allies:

EXERCISE 4

Cultivating Allies Reflection Questions

1. What is my message? (Hint: It's about the institutional bias you've identified.)
2. How will I handle objections and naysayers?
3. How will I communicate my level of commitment?
4. How will I make space for others to participate with me?

The reflection questions from the previous sections should help you gain perspective for questions 1 through 3. The fourth question is very important because it is one of the places that people often alienate potential allies. We can become so obsessed with our own levels of understanding that we belittle those who have not come as far. Remember the work you had to do to earn the credibility to speak and act on the issues you are confronting? Try not to push people away for not having studied the data that you have accessed. Instead, try being a resource and encouraging without being condescending or heavy-handed. Not everyone needs to be an expert on bias to help you achieve your goal of erasing it. Sometimes passion and intent is enough. Sometimes good enough is all we are going to get.

Now, when you find allies who want to dig deep and really entrench themselves in the realities of institutional bias and the historic marginalization of people, awesome! Leverage that to learn more yourself. Don't feel threatened or intimidated by allies who might know more than you do. Be grateful to have them on your team. Remember, diversity of all kinds makes us smarter. And the group is smarter than any individual in it. If you are obsessed with getting all the credit for erasing bias at your institution, just stop now. If you want some kind of medal or glory, you are in it for the wrong reasons and you run the risk of tainting the process. This is a journey for the humble person who is willing to put the needs of other before their own and is willing to share the victory with the village it will take to make the dream a reality.

Step 4: Create a Movement

When you've got a bunch of people dancing with you in the metaphorical park, you've got yourself a movement. A movement is just a group of people who share a collective passion to get something done. Wikipedia defines a social movement as follows:

> *A social movement is a type of group action. Social movements can be defined as organizational structures and strategies that may empower oppressed*

*populations to mount effective challenges and resist
the more powerful and advantaged elites.*

There is nothing insignificant about what we are proposing here. We firmly believe that the collective actions of an intentional group of allies can absolutely affect a change as significant as erasing institutional bias. Our goal is to empower you with the knowledge that breaking the process down into manageable components makes the task surmountable.

We know from our work that there are droves of like-minded people interested in seeing the changes we are discussing. Everyone seems to get hung up on the fact that they can't affect a change alone in a vacuum. Well it's true. They can't. That's why you need to cultivate allies and create a movement. And creating a movement is not nearly as hard as it sounds. Middle-schoolers do it all the time.

Some charismatic kid gets upset about the cafeteria menu. In her mind, the students are oppressed by the disgusting fish sticks they are being served. She gets a bunch of schoolmates on board and they create a petition. She decides to run for student council on a "freedom from fish sticks" platform and enough kids back her that she wins. Charismatic Cathy sets up a meeting with the PTA and pleads her case. Eventually she succeeds and is forever empowered knowing that, with the help of her peers, she got something done.

We mustn't lose our youthful enthusiasm simply because the stakes are higher. We need that enthusiasm even more *because* the stakes are higher. We all have so much more to lose if institutional bias continues to plague our systems and oppress our societies.

Chapter Three

Occupational Bias

In the book that preceded this one, *Overcoming Bias: Building Authentic Relationships across Differences*, the very first exercise we featured was called Job Association. We listed a handful of occupations then left a blank space for people to write the first word or phrase they associated with the named occupation. The examples included teacher, doctor, lawyer, politician, and used-car salesman.

People typically make associations with jobs and job titles. Sometimes they are limited to gender expectations and sometimes, as in the case with used-car salesman or politician, people's assumptions include values-based judgements of character. A great example of this is the oft-told riddle about the man and his son who were in a car accident. The son was badly injured and the father died. When the boy was taken to the emergency room the surgeon said, "I cannot operate on him, he is my son." The question is who is the surgeon? The boy's father died in the car accident. If you don't know the answer we will give you a moment.

. . .

We have watched people spin their wheels on this and come up with everything from, "The boy had two dads, they were a gay couple," to "The dad was resurrected as an angel or a vampire." Have you figured it out yet? Did you guess correctly immediately? The surgeon was the boy's mother. How many of us immediately picture a woman when someone says "surgeon"? Of course, we can argue that all of our biases are rooted in historical facts. In the past, it was uncommon for women to be surgeons, it's true. But we are long past those days and if we don't break those habits of picturing what a job candidate or expert should look like, we will continue to perpetuate cycles of exclusion.

Another example of occupational bias is the often-undervalued role of homemaker and/or stay-at-home parent. Whether male, female, or nonbinary gender–conforming, people tend not to identify work that occurs in the home "real work" unless it's a work-from-home job. Anyone reading this who has been a homemaker or a stay-at-home parent knows exactly what we're talking about. Both of the authors of this book have enjoyed the unique privilege—and the utter insanity—of domestic work. We both agree that it's the hardest job we've ever had. The sleepless nights, the nonstop cleaning, organizing, feeding, chauffeuring, bathing, negotiating, debating . . . it's enough to drive you batty. It's also incredibly rewarding when it's *your* family, and *your* house. One easy litmus test for whether homemaking or stay-at-home parenting is a real job is by asking: *"Would anyone, outside of family, do it for free?"*

Since we all know that the answer is a resounding NO WAY, we will just agree that domestic work is real work and should not be treated as anything different. The reason this matters so much is because when a person decides to re-enter the workplace *out*side the home, the period of domestic work typically counts against them. Why are we penalizing people (most often women, but increasingly other genders) for taking care of their homes and families? Whether it's children, parents, spouse or other family members, shouldn't we value those people *more* highly when they look for traditional employment? The amount of dedication, empathy, organization, care, and compassion required to do those jobs is immeasurable.

People, especially women, are beginning to fear the consequences of motherhood more and more. Some people are choosing not to have children for fear of derailing their careers. That's a massive consequence. Working class families are getting smaller, families are having babies later and later in life. Delays in child-bearing increase the occurrence of birth complications during and after pregnancy. We believe that occupational bias is part of what is driving women to delay growing their families.

Stories like the aforementioned occupational bias that affects homemakers are often easy to empathize with when you or someone close to you has been affected by a similar situation. One of the important aspects of bia work involves seeking out and listening to other people's stories. As you open yourself up to the fullness of the human experience, you will reduce your own bias and its impact on institutions you influence.

Occupational Bias in Tech and Recruiting

A dear friend and personal inspiration of Tiffany Jana's wrote the following when asked how institutional bias has affected her. Andrea Goulet, CEO of the software maintenance tech firm Corgibytes said,

> *The first time I wrote a job description, I noticed that pretty much only men were applying. When I started to dig into why, I realized I was playing into institutional bias in the way I wrote the job description. I actively sought feedback and was able to significantly change the ratio of women on our team. We also required everyone to take unconscious bias training so that we can be aware during recruiting.*

Andrea is a well-established diversity and inclusion champion. She is certainly not the type of person who would set out to exclude people. Nonetheless, her default mode mimicked the behavioral patterns that have been informed by historical institutional bias. What Andrea did correctly was that she investigated the data. She noticed only men were applying so she sought to get to the bottom of why women failed to respond. **The mistake most people make is failing to investigate the data.**

People in organizations typically just notice the phenomenon and either feel helpless to affect a change or feel absolved from any responsibility to do so. People think that since they advertised the job, anyone could have applied. Andrea was open to the idea that maybe something *she was doing* could have contributed to the problem. We need more people to own the idea that it's not just about negligence or failure to do something proactive. Institutional bias can be perpetuated by our actions, patterns, and behaviors regardless of conscious intent.

Moving to solutions in the institutional bias space does not have to be overly complicated. You have to realize that institutional bias is complex, multifaceted, and reinforced by the people and systems that support it, but as long as one person is willing to stare down the problem, name it, and recruit others in an effort to rebuild less biased systems, the obstacles are surmountable. Before we look at how Andrea erased one occupational bias within her organization, let's review the four preliminary steps.

1. **Evaluate your (old) role in perpetuating systemic bias.**
   Andrea came up in the age of engineering where women were in a tiny minority. As a result, the organizational standards were historically developed to accommodate the needs of men. Andrea's behavior defaulted to the established male-oriented standards. She likely perpetuated the male perspective because it was the dominant framework to which she had become accustomed.

2. **Define your (new) role in breaking down systemic bias.**
   Andrea is a born change-maker. She doesn't focus on obstacles, she orients herself toward solutions. She

decided that she could be the one to rewrite the norms and compose a female- and parent-centric narrative. She defined a proactive role in breaking down systemic bias by becoming the person who wrote the new job descriptions and spearheaded women-centric programs in tech environments.

3. Cultivate allies.

As a leader, Andrea is good at getting people on board with ideas. She was able to point out the problem and help people understand her desire to find solutions. She got her team behind her and ran her thoughts by others in the field who acknowledged the validity of the bias issue she had identified.

4. Create a movement.

Andrea became a champion for women's advocacy in tech. She started with her own company and spread her thought leadership throughout the industry by doing keynotes, writing articles, and taking the lead by personally funding initiatives that benefit women and people with children.

These preliminary steps help people get their ducks in a row. It helps ensure that you are personally grounded, invested, and committed to the process. Attempting to erase institutional bias will be exhausting, so you have to do the personal work first. Once you have sufficient support, you can proceed with the following six steps that Andrea took.

EXERCISE 5

Sample *Erasing Institutional Bias* Worksheet

1. Set a clear intention.

Andrea noticed that only men were applying to the jobs she was posting. She decided to take action to see how she could increase the number of women applying and being hired.

2. Lead with data.

Andrea did not have the female representation she wanted, so she set out to sharply increase the percentage of women in her company and in leadership. Her goal was to have 60 percent women in leadership roles.

3. Diagnose accurately.

Andrea could have assumed that women were simply uninterested in the company or the positions she was offering. She knew that there were qualified women in the job market. She knew that she wanted to hire men and women. So she concluded that something her company was doing was preventing women from applying.

4. Deconstruct: eliminate subjective processes.

Andrea examined her actions and realized that her language was inadvertently male-centric. She diagnosed the problem as being one of how the company communicated its needs. The desire to hire women was there, but the supporting behaviors were not present.

5. Reconstruct with objectivity.

Andrea scrubbed the masculine language from the postings and rewrote the job descriptions to be more objective and inclusive.

6. Build in accountability and ongoing measurement.

Andrea maintains a 60 percent female leadership structure and continuously monitors the gender diversity at her company.

Andrea Goulet was fortunate because she is the CEO of Corgibytes. She has the power to make sweeping organizational changes. So what happens if you are an employee who is perhaps not in a leadership position?

Chapter Four

Gender Bias

In the United States, gender is a Title VII protected category for good reason. From the moment women were finally granted access to jobs that were historically reserved for men, they have been taken for granted. Women in the workplace have been underpaid, mistreated, exploited, humiliated, belittled, passed over, and dismissed from the very beginning. While one might expect there to be some friction during the early years of gender integration in the workplace, one would also expect time to smooth out that friction. Yes, women in the workplace have certainly fared better as the decades have rolled on, but women are still compensated less than men, they are still sexually harassed, and they are still massively underrepresented in leadership.

This book is being written by two strong-willed women, so naturally the gender bias discussion comes easily to us. That said, there are plenty of men in the workplace who feel every bit as marginalized as women in certain fields. Male nurses are the first occupation that comes to mind. I've known several male nurses who have to deal with shocked stares when they claim they are nurses instead of doctors. It all goes back to gender stereotypes and perceived gender roles. When society decides that doctors should be men and nurses should be women, anything outside of that is considered awkward and just plain wrong. We place labels on people and occupations and act befuddled when our expectations are not met.

The gender conversation has finally expanded to include gender and gender expression outside of the limiting binary and the gender assigned at birth. While the discussion has expanded and become more inclusive, the structures within organizations have not advanced to kept pace with the times. Organizations are still struggling with how to include all genders—if they are even having the discussion at all.

The Danger of Benevolent Sexism

It's important to also talk about how the equitable treatment of gender minorities in the workplace goes beyond just the elimination of obvious bad behaviors. There are many ways that forms of benevolent sexism can exist and act in the workplace and while these forms of speaking appear on the surface to praise and treasure gender minorities, they are as undermining and damaging to the success and support of gender minorities as more obviously malevolent sexism.

So, what exactly is benevolent sexism? Benevolent sexism works to *compliment* women using stereotypes about them. Benevolent sexism can feel like a favorable attitude toward women but still depends on sexist views of women insofar as women are seen in restricted roles. These feelings are subjectively positive in feeling tone (for the perceiver) and also tend to elicit behaviors typically categorized as prosocial (such as helping) or intimacy seeking: "Women are so much better at being compassionate," or "This office is a mess—you can tell we have too many men in one place." (The implication is that women are neater).[1] Benevolent sexism is present when gender themed events are planned, as a female attorney once described:

> *The women's events at my firm center around makeup and fashion shows rather than substantive, practical training that would help advance our careers.*

Benevolent sexism can go even further, seeking to compliment gender minorities based on stereotypes as well—we've all heard someone say, "I love gay people! They're so well dressed and organized!"

These statements sound harmless enough, right? I mean, we all love to be complimented for things, but most women can tell you about having an experience of being complimented when it sounded nice but felt wrong at the same time. Well, these are clear examples of benevolent sexism—**and while benevolent sexism is often times hard to pinpoint, it's a significant problem both in what it suggests about women, and in the critical role it plays in keeping hostile sexism and inequality in place.**

What do we mean? Benevolent sexism is often subtle. For example, take this satirical rewriting of Albert Einstein's obituary featured in a 2013 article in *Scientific American* on benevolent sexism:

> *He made sure he shopped for groceries every night on the way home from work, took the garbage out, and hand washed the antimacassars. But to his step daughters he was just Dad. "He was always there for us," said his step daughter and first cousin once removed, Margo.*
>
> *Albert Einstein, who died on Tuesday, had another life at work, where he sometimes slipped away to peck at projects like showing that atoms really exist. His discovery of something called the photoelectric effect won him a coveted Nobel Prize.*[2]

The authors of the article note what we all know—it sounds kind of strange, right? If you actually were reading Albert Einstein's real obituary, it would never be written like that. But the same year that the *Scientific American* article was published, rocket scientist Yvonne Bell was given an obituary in the *New York Times* that read as follows:

> *She made a mean beef stroganoff, followed her hus-*
> *band from job to job, and took eight years off from*
> *work to raise three children. "The world's best mom,"*
> *her son Matthew said.*
>
> *But Yvonne Brill, who died on Wednesday at 88 in*
> *Princeton, N.J., was also a brilliant rocket scientist,*
> *who in the early 1970s invented a propulsion system to*
> *help keep communications satellites from slipping out*
> *of their orbits.*[3]

The *New York Times* obituaries editor William McDonald received a tremendous amount of backlash for his memorializing of the brilliant and trailblazing scientist, yet was still unable to see the problem with his copy, which focused on her beef stroganoff and family life. The primary objection raised by readers, though, and the issue that makes this obituary an example of benevolent sexism is the way that Brill's obituary manages to focus on her gender as her primary defining characteristic. Though her scientific achievements are precisely what merited her obituary in the *New York Times* (it's unlikely that they would have written about her just for her beef stroganoff!), the article couched her achievements in terms of gender politics. And this kind of benevolent sexism is not just annoying or inconvenient. It threatens gender equity.

Why is this so? Well, according to Harvard Business School's Research Symposium on Gender and Work,[4] this is because benevolent sexism justifies a traditional power structure of men being dominant and women and gender minorities being secondary and weaker in this hierarchy. Through comments and actions that appear neutral or positive on the surface, but that actually reinforce inequality, women are primarily identified by their gender and constrained by constructed ideas about gender weakness, need, sexuality, and inability. How does this play out in the workplace setting? We'll give you a story for an example.

A friend of ours in the arts shared a story of benevolent sexism mixed with overt sexual harassment. Louise Ricks is an actress, playwright, director, and producer. She said:

> *I was working as a receptionist when a person came in and became very interested in me. They found my professional website and started making comments about my body and what they would like to do with it. They even started calling the office so they could speak to me. They [were] so persistent that I had to call the police. I asked my boss what they were going to do to protect me in the future and they said I should "stop being so cute."*
>
> *[As a result] I don't feel safe working in public spaces anymore. I rarely speak directly with patrons unless I know our interaction is going to be limited. I ended up having to leave my position at that company. I can think of so many examples of how being a young woman has made me feel unsafe in the workplace. This is simply the least vulgar story I can share.*

Louise's story contains a number of concerning things. There's the obvious issue of direct harassment. The client who harassed Louise felt like he had a right to do so, likely because he was flattering her. There's nothing wrong with saying nice things to a woman, right? Wrong. Women are not objects and if they aren't interested in the advances, people need to back off and show some respect.

In addition to this, however, benevolent sexism is clearly happening when Louise asked her employer for help. In this case, the employer actually had a legal obligation to protect Louise. She would have been well within her rights to seek additional support and protection. But when she did, she was told to "stop being so cute." This implies that the harassment was both somehow her fault and also not important enough to be taken seriously.

Louise's employer's example of benevolent sexism is just as toxic as the sexual harassment itself. A 1996 paper written by Peter Glick and Susan Fiske on this form of sexism explains that though the employer may have imagined his words to be a compliment because they drew on traditional masculine stereotyping (that is, that women are to be valued for their appearance and for their utility to men), they actually functioned to marginalize Louise, communicating to her that she was not to be taken seriously.

Glick and Fiske wrote that, "a man's comment to a female coworker on how 'cute' she looks, however well-intentioned, may undermine her feelings of being taken seriously as a professional"[5] For Louise, this response to her complaint not only attacked her professionalism, but her right to demanding safety in her workplace as well.

While these comments have remained hidden in plain sight for decades, the backlash begun in 2017 of toppling high-profile men in the United States from their prominent positions as a result of past harassing behavior toward women is an indication that the tide may be shifting.

When it comes to male–female gender discrimination in the workplace, benevolent sexism does particular damage by supporting environments that cater to patronizing discrimination, "which masquerades as polite help and sympathy while undermining women."[6] Additional research findings published by Glick at Harvard revealed that women overall received less criticism than their male counterparts. Obviously, this was not problematic in and of itself. What was problematic about this trend was that female workers were given less challenging developmental assignments; the study was replicated and the results were the same with thousands of managers. The combination of skewed feedback with less challenging assignments led researchers to conclude that the managers were treating their female employees with kid gloves.[7] This manner of treatment continues to permeate workplaces with the notion that female workers are less capable than their male counterparts.

Sarah Miller, another friend of ours, currently works in senior management at a large international nongovernmental organization (NGO). Sarah is responsible for overall organizational development and accountability with a specific focus on gender inequality and women and girls' empowerment. Yet even in her field, where gender equality is an institutional priority, Sarah has experienced the reality that benevolent sexism often remains, even when a workplace is "fair" on the surface.

I was about 26 years old, just starting out in my career after graduate school, and was noticed after about a year by the COO. He seemed to feel I had potential, and would call me in to meetings to observe along with other more senior colleagues.

As time went on, I began to take on increasing responsibility and was able to share my ideas and contribute to group projects more actively. Our COO acted "proud" of me—in a way that a parent would be proud of their child. He would exclaim over my contributions, and point out things I did well, and smile and nod when I spoke up. He always called me terms like "sweetie" or "kiddo." I felt as though I was regularly being patted on the head, like a young girl being praised for doing well, rather than a peer exchanging valued ideas.

It was noticeably different than the way my young male colleagues were acknowledged. They were appreciated, but in a way that was asking what was expected of them and treated more directly and exactingly, as equals. And it also felt necessary for me to slide into the role of the young, inexperienced, naïve, and grateful tutee, if I wanted to continue to get into the inner fold, seen and valued as an "up and coming" bright young professional.

This went on for about two years, and when he left to become the CEO of another organization I remember feeling relieved that I didn't have to play that part anymore.

Sarah shared her experience with other female colleagues and found that they, too, had found themselves feeling a similar vague discomfort and an unspoken demand than they play a role. Even those who weren't his subordinates experienced this. Sarah wrote:

One of my colleagues who was a senior manager and peer of his at the time described it as feeling forced to act flighty, in need of his help and grateful for his leadership and assistance, in order to get things done through him. She actively did so, very aware of what she was doing but felt it was a necessary way of "working the system." I usually felt slimy, which was odd looking back because there was nothing even remotely sexual or inappropriate. But it bothered me. Not actively, not in a way that disrupted my work or upset me, but in a way that was there under the surface, causing me to internally cringe and then quickly gear up for any interaction with him, sliding into this "cute,

young, trying hard but a little helpless if it wasn't for
this nice big man looking out for me" character.

As we discussed in the content on stereotype threats, this kind of experience detracts from our ability to be fully present in a workplace. As Sarah says, it was "there under the surface," causing her to expend energy working to adjust to it. Not only was Sarah's COO operating with clearly gendered and patronizing posture toward her and other female colleagues, but he was also demanding that they make subtle psychological adjustments in order to work within his framework. They had to play the part of the grateful young tutee, or the helpless employee who was lucky to get support.

Sarah's work has spanned more than a decade now in global poverty work and in response to this experience, she has mentored and made space for young women to move up in the field. Sarah's intention has been to empower those young women to avoid experiences like the one that she had.

I speak [to these young women] directly about the ways
in which they should be firm in negotiating pay, in the
terms of their contracts, in what they should expect
from the organization and the people in it. And I am
able to influence policy and systems with open eyes,
and be clear when I am not okay with male colleagues
defaulting to roles such as expecting females to be the
note takers, and actively ask them to step up. I can
do these things because I am in a senior role now. But
the status quo is still there, I'm just not willing to play
the part.

Benevolent sexism is a tricky target but an important one in this day and age when we know what *not* to say and do, but we

45

sometimes get confused about how to move forward. This manner of speaking about women and other gender minorities, however, is a wrong turn that leads to further marginalization and discrimination precisely because it assumes essential identifying facts about groups of people based on only one aspect about them. *All* women aren't better at being compassionate than *all* men—that's impossible! And *all* gay people aren't well-dressed and organized!

Sexism in the workplace is a horrific threat to equality, but it's important to understand that benevolent sexism can act as a false solution to hostile sexism. We have worked with countless clients who have heard "We love women!" in a job interview only to find that once in the workplace, their gender is still their primary identifier.

Maternity Bias in the Workplace

Nathalia Artus, a community development professional in the banking industry, describes her experience witnessing maternity bias:

> *Sometimes the motherhood bias starts even before a woman has a baby. Once the woman gets engaged, it definitely starts. In my previous office, that was a constant conversation. The conversation was followed by the act of eliminating candidates from the succession pool if they had kids or were of child-bearing age.*

The type of bias Nathalia describes is an unacceptable employment practice. Organizations are not permitted to deny women professional opportunities based on their gender. The ability or decision to get pregnant is a factor limited to women and is therefore a sex-based issue.

Pregnancy, engagement, and being of child-bearing age are not related to professional competency and should *never* be factored into how women are rated, promoted, evaluated, or advanced within an organization. Women are literally populating the planet and proliferating the human species. Punishing females of childbearing age for upholding their reproductive purpose is kind of crazy. What's worse is referring to a woman's return from the maternity transition as a "comeback." This is another example of benevolent sexism. What is she coming back from? She wasn't hit by a car, she was making another human. Pregnancy and motherhood are not disabilities, so the associated rites of passage should not be treated as liabilities or inconveniences.

We have heard the argument that women should be paid less than men because they might get pregnant and take maternity leave. Again, this is short-sighted thinking. Women work just as hard as men and tend to be more loyal to organizations that don't penalize them for choosing to grow their families. Assuming that women cannot have children *and* a career robs women and their families of basic human dignity and respect.

Raising children is no longer relegated to "women's work" and men are not the only gender deserving of thriving professional careers. Treat people as human beings with the right to grow their careers and families in equal measure. Promote and assign based on technical and interpersonal competencies. Leave people's reproductive lives out of your professional decision matrix.

The same applies for families who adopt. The decision to adopt is their business, and unless your organization is planning to enthusiastically support adoptive families, their parental status is off-limits as a professional variable.

So, what can you do about gender bias if you care enough to act? Well, a lot, it turns out, and our six steps conform with what analysis and studies have demonstrated. The first step is raising your awareness—sexism in all its forms is significantly dangerous.

Benevolent sexism contributes to the danger and acceptance of hostile sexism in significant ways, and the presence of benevolent sexism has significant consequences in and of itself! Furthermore, the best way to deal with benevolent sexism seems to be attacking hostile sexism as well!

Researchers with Harvard Business School's Research Symposium reported again that the correlation between hostile sexism and benevolent sexism in both workplace and domestic settings was a big one for women. When women live in nations where the threat of direct, hostile sexism is significant and they report that fear to researchers, those same women tend to endorse benevolent sexism, and are more accepting of a patronizing structure of working and living.[8] But when the threat of hostile sexism is less—when women can work and live and thrive without fearing the violence of hostile sexism—then women can reject benevolent sexism and enjoy the same freedom and flexibility as men. The work of erasing institutional bias, getting data, and creating systems of accountability is actually what is called for!

Intersectionality—When Marginalized Identities Comingle and Amplify Bias

We want to take a moment to address intersectionality before we share an example of someone using the six steps to address gender bias. "Intersectionality" is the idea that systems of oppression such as sexism, racism, and other forms of discrimination intersect and are not mutually exclusive.

Kimberlé Crenshaw first coined the theory of intersectionality while simultaneously, over the course of several years, finding herself, as an African American women, a talking point in the dissection of the concept. In her work, Crenshaw argues that the experiences of being a woman of color cannot be recognized in terms of being black and a woman independently. These experiences in discrimination instead need to be considered as a sum in order to fully address the bias that women of color face on a daily basis.

Lisa Crawson (name changed to protect her privacy) shared her experience as a female executive who addressed an intersectional institutional bias:

In several small businesses (40–100 employees), there were no formal yearly evaluations. In these particular businesses, all supervisors were white and majority were male. The office receptionist, accountants, legal assistants, and/or medical billers were mostly minority women while the personal assistants were white women. Then you add in what I call the "back office curse."

Leaders never approach these staff members with good news and thanks. They were quick to point out errors. It's like the electric company—no one says thanks for running well and keeping the lights on— they just get screamed at if there is no power.

It was perceived by the receptionist, medical billers, legal assistants, and accountants that the leaders had no understanding or appreciation of their daily contributions to the company or cared about their careers. This was due to the absence of a performance development system and appraisal system. It was easy for these staff to question whether it may have something to do with being a minority. I have seen this many times in my career and it makes me sad.

When I approach the leaders about staff feeling "invisible," they usually say they do not know what to

*say or how to start a simple conversation or they do
not want to go "around the chain of command."*

*In all cases, I was able to help the status quo. I
met with staff, learned what they liked and did not
like about their current jobs, or listened to their process issues. I tried to find solutions. Then we talked
about their personal goals. I then scheduled trainings
and/or informal mixers with department leaders.*

*In one case, I invited the CEO to a bowling outing
and introduced him one-by-one to each of the staff
and gave him a personal detail about each. He was a
naturally engaging, fun guy. All the staff had one-on-
one time with him and each side felt at ease and
appreciated. The difference was amazing.*

*Another time, I implemented new systems, but had
staff do all the manager training and run the help
desk. It gave them an opportunity to demonstrate their
knowledge and be a valued resource for leaders of the
company.*

What we love about Lisa's story was that she took action
when she saw a problem. Many of us see the problems, but that's
the end of it. Notice the feeling language Lisa uses, ". . . it makes
me sad." What we like to share with people we work with is the
fact that when you *feel* something about a particular circum-
stance, that is your call to action.

When something at work or in the media or in your life
makes your stomach ball up, pay attention. When something
makes you uncomfortable, upset, or even angry—listen to that.
That is a visceral reaction telling you that something matters and
needs your attention.

Some people respond to animal issues that way, some people don't. It takes all kinds of people to help keep the world in balance. We can't all be animal activists and aficionados. We don't all need to be. So if human inequity just doesn't affect you one tiny bit, perhaps it's not your fight. But if any part of you shudders when people are mistreated, left out, pushed aside, passed over, or worse—abused—then you are being called by humanity to offer some form of assistance.

This is what the six steps are for. Let us help you organize your effort into something actionable, impactful, and sustainable. Let's continue and see how many of the six steps Lisa described and fill in any missing steps with recommendations for sustainability.

1. **Set a clear intention.**

   Lisa wanted to help the back-office team feel more included and valued.

2. **Lead with data.**

   Lisa noted that the demographics of the supervisors were all white males, the assistants were white females, and the remaining support staff was minority women. Job descriptions are no longer legally permitted to include race and gender, so some sort of bias was clearly at play to create such consistent racial and gender divisions by job classification and seniority.

3. **Diagnose accurately.**

   Lisa did not assume she understood the behaviors and circumstances that caused the back-office staff to feel marginalized. She engaged in a qualitative research process by meeting with them and listening to their experiences.

4. Deconstruct: eliminate subjective processes.

Lisa disrupted the status quo by lowering the invisible wall between the back-office staff and the front office. In the absence of objective facts, people typically fill in the blanks with assumptions. Lisa's story includes several descriptors that illuminate how the front office felt about the back office and/or how the back office felt they were perceived:

- Unappreciated
- Invisible
- Misunderstood
- Unintelligent

She helped lower the invisible wall by creating opportunities for the two offices to interact outside of the awkwardly segregated work environment. Social mixers and the bowling event allowed the colleagues to experience each other as humans. We have long held that the biggest reason professional relationships are so vacuous and transactional is the result of people failing to see each other as fully human at work.

It's easier to have compassion and passion with your family and friends than with colleagues. Even when family and friends prove challenging, you maintain a vested interest in sustaining the relationship in the long term, and you often have history and context for those close relationships that cause them to be more resilient than workplace relationships.

We mustn't forget that colleagues are people, too. Failing to see them as human and treat them as the precious people that they are is a failure of our own humanity. We look to their flaws and differences as justifications for our distance, but that is shortsighted and unkind.

The reality is that humans function in a symbiotic manner. If one person's stress levels are high in a group, it stresses everyone else out. The inverse is also true. People love being on teams with joy-filled, kind, energetic people because that energy doesn't drag you down. It's contagious and uplifting. This is why the best thing for all of us is to lift up and take care of each other.

5. Reconstruct with objectivity.

Lisa instituted new objective systems to combat the old ones that allowed room for subjective assumptions. She created trainings that allowed the full staff to participate on equal footing, and implemented systems that allowed the back office to demonstrate their knowledge and institutional value. Inviting the back office to manage the new systems disrupted the marginalizing status quo by providing objective evidence that they were knowledgeable, intelligent, informed, and valuable to the organization.

6. Build in accountability and ongoing measurement.

Lisa's organization chose to apply for a Best Places to Work award. This meant that staff had to complete a survey every year. They received a very good overall score, but they had issues with morale which was affecting hiring and recruiting, so it was a great way to address both issues. The survey is available online so it was easy for management to look at and really reflect on what they were doing right or wrong and address any issues. Lisa reviewed the survey with the partners and each of them come to their own realization about how poorly they were communicating and managing staff. Identifying a tool to use for ongoing measurement is a very good way to leverage objective metrics for ongoing accountability.

Chapter Five

Diversity is a workplace and organizational buzzword that we all love to throw around, right? We know it's important, maybe we're not always entirely sure why. It just seems good to have different people in an organizational setting, particularly people whose racial and ethnic backgrounds are different.

No one wants to think that her or his workplace is racially charged. When it comes to creating a healthy culture of racial diversity and inclusion, though, the actual demands of doing this are less sexy than the glossy brochure idea of a diverse setting. In other words, if you really want to create a healthy, racially diverse workplace, you are going to find yourself face-to-face with the often hidden but appallingly powerful grip of institutional racial bias and its impact on organizational environments.

We totally get it—no one wants to raise his or her hand and claim part in perpetuating racial biases. The difficult truth, however, is that we have long been culturally conditioned in many ways to find it unbelievable that we ourselves might be part of the problem.

In 2016, *New York Times* reporter Greg Howard wrote a powerful brief explaining how we are culturally socialized to see only individualized racism as an issue. If we aren't "being racist," then things should be fine, right? Howard's account explained that our current understanding of racism—the one that situates racism most prominently in the individual human heart rather than in institutional practices and policies like gerrymandering, racial profiling, educational systems, or the drug war—came about during the civil-rights era and was actually exemplified by George Wallace of Alabama.

Wallace, in trying to differentiate between a racist and a segregationist said that, "A racist is one who despises someone because of his color, and an Alabama segregationist is one who conscientiously believes that it is in the best interest of the Negro and white to have separate educational and separate order."[1] That is to say, racism is the distinct act of individual people with hate in their hearts, but the segregationist just believes that these separate systems make things better for everyone involved.

Why is this story about George Wallace relevant to the work of institutional bias today? Well, we share this story to illustrate the reality that for decades, white Americans have been prone to characterize racism as an individual problem that *other* people have. However, the perpetuation of racism has virtually always been supported most heavily by policies, institutions, and systems. Additionally, we are culturally conditioned against seeing the ways that bias works. For example, look at our criminal justice system. People tend to turn a blind eye to the bias-based injustice that befalls people our society deems unworthy or deserving of punishment. Why are African Americans six times more likely to be prosecuted on drug-related charges than white people in the United States when white people are more than four times more likely to use drugs than African Americans?[2] Because African Americans are more likely to be profiled and stopped in the United States, and are therefore more likely to be caught.

In addition to disparities in drug-related charges, a 2014 study found that African Americans are incarcerated at more than five times the rate of whites and constitute 34 percent of the 6.8 million correctional population.[3] These are well-documented statistics with associated biased behaviors that persist because we do not have enough people who are actively concerned about the well-being of potential criminals.

Biased behavior affects virtually all aspects of life for marginalized groups. It is hard enough to get support to change the status quo for outcomes like infant mortality and workplace discrimination, that getting buy-in to create fair, humane, and equitable treatment for people who have broken the law feels like a long shot. Nonetheless, it is one we will address in chapter[8].

George Wallace was one of our nation's icons of racist rhetoric, perpetuating the institution of racist systems as he fought to uphold full-scale segregation in Alabama in the 1960s. Despite his open endorsement of these systems, though, his self-understanding may not be that far off from the self-understanding of many white Americans today. In other words, as Wallace's thinking saw other individuals as the enemy, he himself was actually pushing systems that caused violence to black Americans.

Wallace worked to publicly distinguish himself from a true racist by explaining true racism as a problem of intention and heart—a problem he declared he simply did not have. Interestingly, the first Prime Minister and President of Ghana, Kwame Nkrumah once posited that racist policies actually create racist ideas—not necessarily the other way around. If we keep thinking of racism as the work of only isolated, terrible, bad, racist people, then the systems as a whole (the systems that are causing racialized outcomes, such as education, criminal justice, health, and economic systems) don't need to be reimagined, only individuals need to be reformed. We are stuck believing that institutional racial bias is a thing of the past, something that ended with the introduction of civil rights and was eliminated with the death of Jim Crow.

There are many issues with that kind of thinking, but one of the most crippling organizational issues that we come across happens this way: when leaders miss this particular mark on institutional bias, particularly when it comes to race, and it translates into overconfidence in their ability to work across demographics, it actually then results in a reduced capacity to truly achieve diversity and inclusion in an organization. We see this evidenced when we conduct organizational assessments. We often ask people to indicate the degree to which they agree with the following statements:

- I have confidence in my ability to interact with people who are different than me (culturally, ethnically, gender, etc.).
- I have confidence in my colleagues' ability to interact with people who are different than me (culturally, ethnically, gender, etc.).

Much of the time, many people we work with overestimate their own abilities to interact across demographic differences and underestimate their colleagues' ability to do the same. Rarely do people see themselves as part of the problem. Even when the problem is evident to people across the organization, it is a rare institution that is populated with individuals willing or able to accept their role in the creation and maintenance of biased systems.

People tend to believe that everyone else is the problem, that the need for reform lies outside of themselves and just in other individuals who need a change of heart. In fact, our experience has been further confirmed by data recently released in research published by leadership consulting firm Zenger/Folkman in *Harvard Business Review*. In analyzing ten years of data about feedback of over 1.5 million raters describing 122,000 leaders, the firm found that the higher a leader rates him- or herself on valuing diversity and practicing inclusion, the more likely those leaders are to overrate their effectiveness.

Additionally, those who are rated the best by their employees don't realize their skill and capability. Their conclusion? "While a person's effectiveness with any skill always needs to be based on the evaluations of others, rather than self-perception, it seems especially true in this case. You might intend to be inclusive, and even think you are inclusive, but your impact on others might be very different."[4] In other words, when you read bias as an individual problem that you don't have rather than a systemic issue that requires collaborative work to dismantle, you become part of the problem instead of an ally for change. More importantly, this kind of thinking leaves the truest racialized obstacles and problems that perpetuate inequality and injustice intact. We are still living in a society where African Americans face higher unemployment rates, lower life expectancy rates, and higher incarceration rates.

We still struggle to cultivate relationships of trust in our organizations and workplaces. We still see boardrooms where black men and women are significantly underrepresented. The racial wealth gap has continued to far outpace the slightly improved income gap between blacks and whites, as white households own, on average, seven times as much wealth as African American households and six times as much as Latino households. At current growth rates, it would take black Americans 228 years to have as much wealth as white Americans have today.[5]

When racism is understood as a multidimensional and highly adaptive system—a system that ensures an unequal distribution of resources between racial groups—rather than an individual feeling lodged in individual hearts, then we can begin to attack these sorts of inequalities and the systems that have long ensured that these outcomes continue.

Avoiding the Conversation Does Not Help

Many leaders report that they are anxious or uncomfortable raising issues of racial bias or even publicly addressing racial incidents that are in the national news cycle. Some are uncomfortable because they believe these are individual issues. Some worry that differing views will create unnecessary organizational conflict. Leaders sometimes simply don't know what to say.

We want to challenge that. Though it may not be your intention, giving in to discomfort and anxiety and avoiding hard conversations can actually sustain a biased environment. In the short run, it only benefits those who have traditionally held power. In the long run, it's actually not good for anyone. Even organizations that have worked hard to recruit minority employees risk missing out on countless opportunities for proven positive growth when they fail to do the hard and at times painful work of addressing institutional bias. So, what happens when we don't address issues of institutional racial bias at an organizational level?

Harvard Business School's Center for Talent Innovation set out to answer this question and other related questions. They started by taking a look at what kind of impact our political, social, and racial experiences have on job contributions. Their nationwide survey of 3,570 white-collar professionals revealed that for black, Asian, and Hispanic professionals, race-based discrimination is rampant outside of workplace settings.[6] Of the black professionals surveyed, 78 percent said they've experienced discrimination or fear that they or their loved ones will. And yet, of those surveyed, 38 percent said that they feel it's never acceptable at their companies to speak out or share about their experience of bias.

Researchers linked this silence to feelings of isolation and alienation in the workplace. Black employees who feel unable to speak about their experiences are nearly three times as likely as those who feel comfortable sharing to have one foot out the door, and they are 13 times as likely to be disengaged in their workplaces. These employees report that they feel unable to bring their whole selves to work.[7]

In addition to negative repercussions in the workplace, unexamined institutional racial bias carries with it even more potentially catastrophic consequences for those subject to these biases.

Researchers at University of California, Berkeley, are studying how, in their words, racism "gets under the skin."[8] These scientists have been asking how persistent exposure to institutional bias may impact health outcomes, even when differences in income and education are taken into account. While it's still in its early stages, the correlations are clear between frequent experiences of discrimination and decreased health outcomes. Amani Nuru-Jeter, a social epidemiologist working on the project, says:

> *Prolonged elevation [and] circulation of the stress hor-*
> *mones in our bodies can be very toxic and compromise*
> *our body's ability to regulate key biological systems*
> *like our cardiovascular system, our inflammatory sys-*
> *tem, our neuroendocrine system . . . It just gets us*
> *really out of whack and leaves us susceptible to a*
> *bunch of poor health outcomes.*[9]

For example, researchers discovered that these stress reactions can occur with even the expectation of a racist encounter. This persistent stress is associated with chronic low-grade inflammation—a little like having a low fever all the time, which dysregulates the body in a way that, over time, could put someone at a higher risk for a condition like heart disease.[10]

Creating a workplace or organizational culture that normalizes dealing with institutional bias, rather than implicitly forcing its employees to internalize bias, can change this. It can even be considered an important part of wellness and stress management that is still being neglected despite companies funding significant fitness and health initiatives across the country. In other words, if you and your company value employee physical health and workplace well-being, then doing the work to process institutional bias is actually part of that well-being.

Becca Carter describes her experience as an African American female executive at a large financial institution:

> *I am the first African American to be in a leadership role in my company. It is frustrating to feel less respected, always having to prove myself, and like I am being watched.*
>
> *When I make a decision as a leader in charge of $3 million budget, I get asked by others if my boss has ok'd my decision. People hired off the streets that don't look like me, don't get asked this same question. I have been there over 15 years.*

Becca is describing a situation that results in massive amounts of stress and anxiety for people of color in particular. It would be easy for a friend or colleague to attribute her experience to gender, personality, or some other variable. After 15 years at the same institution, Becca has experienced a pattern of microaggressions, the seemingly insignificant but hurtful slights we will discuss in our next section. She has also experienced enough bias to be able to isolate her race as the basis for the unequal treatment she receives. There are other women executives in her office. There are also other African Americans. Her general experience is more aligned with that of the other nonmanagement African Americans than the white women in management.

Microaggressions

Unfortunately, the themes and experiences found in Becca's story are ones we consistently hear when talking with people about their experiences with institutional bias. Another consistent theme throughout Becca's story, and many others are cases, is microaggression. "Microaggressions" can be defined as everyday exchanges that send disparaging messages to individuals due to their personal demographic identities. The patterns of being second-guessed and feeling less respected are microaggressions that Becca receives from her company's leadership.

Some microaggressions can be more overt than others. Completing a lengthy project, feeling full of pride and accomplishment, only to be told "I never would have guessed *you* would have done so well" can completely negate any positive emotions that come with successfully meeting a deadline. When a new hire is making small talk with a coworker and is asked, "Where are you from? No, I mean, where you are *really* from," can have lasting effects on personal and professional dynamics with someone you're expected to collaborate with on a daily basis. It can be off-putting, to say the least, when you are on the receiving end of these remarks. Below are some intervention styles as well as examples of ways to incorporate them into your interactions with others. Like any change, systemic change starts with the small interventions individuals can instigate without anyone else's input or permission.

MICROAGGRESSION WORKSHEET[11]

INTERVENTION STYLE

Microaggression intervention

Inquire

Ask the speaker to elaborate. This will give you more information on where they are coming from and may help the speaker understand what they are saying.

To a person of color:

"I don't believe in race . . . "

"So, what do you believe in? Can you elaborate more on that?"

To a person of Asian descent:

"You all are good at math. Can you help me with this problem?"

"Can you elaborate more on that?"

"I heard you say that all Asians are good at math. What makes you believe that?"

Reframe

Create a different way to look at the situation.

To a woman of color:

"I would have never guessed you are a scientist."

"I'm wondering what message this is sending her. Do you think you would have said this to a white male?"

Paraphrase & reflect

Reflect back to the speaker the essence of what they said. This demonstrates an understanding and reduces defensiveness by both you and the speaker.

"Everyone can succeed in this society if they work hard enough."

"So, you feel that everyone can succeed in this society if they work hard enough. Have you met any hardworking people who struggle to make ends meet?"

Preference statements

Clearly communicate a preference rather than stating them as demands or having others guess what needs to happen.

Talking over a woman in a group of all men.

Someone makes a racist, sexist, or homophobic joke.

"I would like to participate, but I need you to let me finish my thought."

"I didn't think that was funny and I would like you to stop."

Revisit

Even if the moment has passed, go back and address the micro-aggression. Research indicates an unaddressed microaggression can leave just as much of a negative impact as the microaggression itself.

To a woman:

"Of course he'll get tenure, he's a minority!"

"Let's rewind for a moment to what you just said yesterday. You said you believe that he will get tenure just because of his race. I thought it was inappropriate and wanted to check in with you."

Considerations:

- The communication approaches are most effective when used in combination with one another, e.g., using impact and preference statements, using inquiry and paraphrasing together, etc.
- Separate the person from the action or behavior. Instead of saying "you're racist", try saying "that could be perceived as a racist remark." Being called a racist puts someone on the defensive and can be considered "fighting words."
- Avoid starting questions with "Why"—it puts people on the defensive. Instead try "how" "what made you . . ."
- When addressing a microaggression, try to avoid using the pronoun "you" too often—it can leave people feeling defensive and blamed. Use "I" statements describing the impact on you instead or refer to the action indirectly, e.g., "when _____ was said..." or "when _____ happened . . ."
- How you say it is as critical as what you say, e.g., tone of voice, body language, etc. The message has to be conveyed with respect for the other person, even if one is having a strong negative reaction to what's been said. So it is helpful to think about your intention when interrupting a microaggression—e.g., do you want that person to understand the impact of his/her action, or stop his/her behavior, or make the person feel guilty, etc. Your intention and the manner in which you execute your intention make a difference.
- Sometimes humor can defuse a tense situation.

Attributional Ambiguity

Finding yourself on the receiving end of alienating comments and unfounded assumptions can lead to more existential concerns in oneself: Why are these things happening to me? These feelings are known as "attributional ambiguity." We touched on this subject in *Overcoming Bias,* but here is a brief refresher:

Attributional ambiguity is a concept that describes how hard it can be to determine why bad things are happening to you. Basically, it means that when you are a member of a marginalized group, you never know whether something happens to you because you are a member of that group or whether it just happened randomly.

A university professor shared the following disheartening story with us. In her case, as in many, she was unable to instigate systemic change. She used some of the steps, but was not successful in using all six. See if you can tell what went wrong.

I noted that students of color were retaining at my institution at least 10 percentage points behind white students. To me this was evidence of something that I had suspected from my student interactions—that the climate for students of color was poor. When I mentioned this to institutional decision makers, I was told that it's because they aren't as prepared for college and/or they have troubles paying tuition past the first year.

I returned to the data to answer this question. I controlled for high school GPA and for financial unmet need, and the race variable was still the most powerful. It was simply their "student of color" status, not financial ability or high school preparation, that mattered to whether they stayed. Further, I found other data that the college had been collecting for years where students of color rated the quality of their peer interaction much lower than the white students did. In other words, white students liked students on campus much more than students of color did.

I approached decision makers with this insight, and they seemed interested, but didn't change anything about their approach. They consistently seemed nervous to do anything to improve the community for students of color due to the concern for making white students uncomfortable. Because white students' comfort mattered more.

I was furious. I kept talking about it to whomever would listen. I wanted to inspire a group of informed allies who could help impact change. I came to realize that I was being viewed as unprofessional. I experienced an "ah-ha" moment. We've come to define "professionalism" in part as upholding the current oppressive systems. Speaking truth about our current biased systems is viewed unprofessional!? That was a gut punch.

I do not believe I was able to change the status quo at that institution, though some may point to a few small initiatives that the school started. The efforts seemed nominal and not likely to affect real change. Ultimately, I left the institution. Frankly, I had the feeling that my days were numbered there anyway. In that instance, I felt that the system was much stronger than I was.

The professor was off to a great start before things went awry. It's important for us to learn from our failures as well as our successes. Unfortunately, in the work of unraveling systemic bias, failure is likely if we don't stay the course. This is only because the status quo of accepted or ignored institutional bias is failure. Let's look at what happened on the professor's journey.

1. Set a clear intention.

She was attempting to improve the scores, retention, and college experience for students of color.

2. Lead with data.

The professor used data to make her case. She noted consistent differences in scores, retention, and experiences with peers correlated to race.

3. Diagnose accurately.

The professor relied on more than one data set. She collected her own data and cross-referenced it with data that the institution was already collecting. She controlled for several variables to increase the validity of her hypothesis.

4. Deconstruct: eliminate subjective processes.

The professor was unable to secure sufficient buy-in from leadership to deconstruct the biased processes.

5. Reconstruct with objectivity.

This step was not possible without the prerequisite deconstruction.

6. Build in accountability and ongoing measurement.

The university never got to this step because everything stalled at step four. What went wrong?

The professor fell short in the preliminary work. Remember the four steps we discussed in chapter 1?

1. Evaluate your (old) role in perpetuating systemic bias.
2. Define your (new) role in breaking down systemic bias.
3. Cultivate allies.
4. Create a movement.

The professor had not thoroughly evaluated her role nor clearly defined her new role in breaking down systemic bias at the university. Any work related to diversity, equity, and inclusion requires a substantial amount of self-work. One cannot be optimally effective without first gazing introspectively at your own strengths and blind spots.

Perhaps her biggest mistake was failing to secure allies before approaching leadership with the problem. Leaders don't want problems, they want solutions. And if you are presenting something as substantial and potentially damning as evidence of institutional bias, you'd better have a cohort or an army of likeminded people who see the problem.

Why isn't it enough to be able to prove the problem to leadership? It's not enough because of the people who benefit from the oppression imposed through unchecked bias. Leaders are also not always quick to claim culpability for failure. Without a team of allies to back you up, you run the risk of looking like a crazy person. One person is far more easily dismissed and shoved aside than a large group. Had the professor's entire department or a critical mass of her peers, and perhaps students, been on board, the impact would have been much different. This is also why the discernment questions in Exercise 2 are so critical. You have to understand your stakeholders and how they are affecting and affected by institutional bias.

The consequences of *not* addressing institutional racial bias are significant but there is good news about what happens when you do begin to enter the work of erasing racial bias in your workplace.

The Center for Talent Innovation released further data which painted an encouraging picture of the possibilities that arise when organizations begin to talk about difficult issues of race. They concluded that talking about race at work actually benefits the business! Rather than distracting employees from business, companies' efforts to respond to and address race eliminate distraction by kicking the proverbial and truly distracting elephant out of the room.

Additionally, CTI found that among respondents who knew of companies responding to societal incidents of racial discrimination or bias, the vast majority of those respondents said that the response made them view the company in a more positive way. Put more plainly, the brand actually benefits when the company talks honestly about race, gender, and bias.[12]

It's important to be *very clear* that diversity itself isn't the complete answer to erasing racial bias and data is going to be a flexible concept if you want to address the nature of what is happening in your organizational context with authenticity. Many organizations, though, complain that they have tried and still can't figure out why they have a diversity problem or why they struggle to keep diverse employees.

These same organizations often worry that the mechanisms that are being applied to address bias issues—evidence-based people analytics, for example—are dependable only when there are enough people in the relevant sample size. In other words, according to Maxine Williams, Facebook's Global Head of Diversity, these companies are saying, "if only there were more of you, we could tell why there are so few of you."[13]

In a widely circulated 2017 article entitled "Numbers Only Take Us So Far,"[14] Williams suggests that companies and analysts should regularly push themselves to look beyond the hard data. This is especially important when those minority numbers are small either because an organization is significantly white and male, or the organization is a smaller sized one in general because **"Statistics don't capture what it feels like to be the only black team member."**[15]

She argues that we don't have to prove that there is a bias operating in performance reviews or hiring processes, for example. In other words, we don't have to reinvent the statistical wheel in our own company settings because so much data has already been generated. The breadth and depth of social science research has already done that work for us, so we can begin to operate as though bias exists in our companies. We can then do the work of really listening to our minority employees—this is gathering of "descriptive data"—and then we can use this data to examine the impact of bias on the ground.[16]

Williams advocates strongly for both a qualitative and quantitative lens on bias—the statistics and the stories—but if your organization is in a position where the quantitative lens is challenged by numbers, then learn from what is out there and listen to the employees who are in your organization. This is data! We'd like to share the story of one CEO's journey with racial bias that reflects Williams' advice and does the work of erasing systemic bias.

In the first few days of July 2016, racially charged gun violence was occurring at an overwhelming pace. Philando Castile was shot and killed by police in St. Louis, Alton Sterling was shot and killed by police in Baton Rouge, and five Dallas police officers were shot and killed at a Black Lives Matter rally.

For employees at PricewaterhouseCoopers (PwC), the emotional toll was heavy. While many white employees felt confused about the conversation on race, black employees felt like they *couldn't* talk about it at work. US CEO Tim Ryan was only a few days into his new role and sent out a company-wide email addressing the most recent string of events and asking how folks were coping. After sending the email on Friday, July 8th, his inbox was flooded with responses from minority employees that overwhelmingly said,"*When I came to work today, the silence was deafening.*"

In the over two hundred emails that Ryan received, employees communicated that *not* talking about the national events was creating a disconnect from their actual experiences in the world, and made the workplace challenging in numerous ways. And while PwC already had a number of initiatives on diversity and inclusion, they were somehow missing the mark in terms of opening the way for minority employees to bring their whole selves into the workplace where they spent a significant amount of time.

Ryan explained that, "It might seem misplaced to get this personal at work. It's definitely unusual in corporate America. But having these kinds of deep discussions, opening up about how you're doing, is simply an acknowledgement that work is where we spend a lot of our time."[18] People should be able to be comfortable, should be able to feel that their voices are heard. And from a boss or supervisor's perspective, people do their best work when they feel heard and valued.

In a post on LinkedIn detailing the company's first steps to talk openly about race, Ryan described how the reaction to his email "brought home the depth and immediacy of how deeply this situation is affecting PwC employees, and how much they wanted to connect with others to process what was unfolding."[19] Ryan scrapped his new CEO 100-day plan and set to work collaborating with teammates in PwC to hold company-wide open and transparent conversations about race on July 21.

These meetings, called "ColorBrave: A Conversation About Race," were informal with no agenda. In order to preserve privacy, they were not filmed, and employees were asked to keep what was discussed in the room private. The conversations were initiated by Ryan and Elena Richards, a representative from PwC's office, and people were given space to just talk. The meetings were uncomfortable at times. Employees shared stories of being afraid for themselves or their families, of struggling with fear of the police. Employees bluntly expressed that they felt invisible at work. Marvin Washington, a partner at PwC, shared that what impacted him the most was the response from white leadership. "They're like, 'Wow, I had no idea people felt this way, that they were going through these things.'"[20]

Before we reveal how Tim Ryan and PwC are moving forward after these conversations, let's see how what they are doing works to erase institutional bias.

1. Set a clear intention.

Tim Ryan's hope for his employees was that they realize their full potential. He realized early on that if they were unable to communicate with one another about a significant part of their lived experience—namely, the racialized violence happening all around them—then everyone would struggle.

2. Lead with data.

The emails that Ryan received in the days following the shootings confirmed that employees were not able to thrive in the climate at PwC, particularly because they were unable to talk openly about difficult issues related to race. This data would meet Maxine Williams' description of data as the sort that demonstrates the impact of bias on the ground.

3. Diagnose accurately.

Following the response to the initial email, Ryan announced that he wanted to hear more and have employees hear more from one another, though the prospect caused a great deal of alarm. "The response both inside and outside the firm was 'Oh my God,' says Ryan. 'They worried that it would all go off the rails and turn into a fight about right and wrong and the police,' he says."[21]

But in order to actually hear from *all* his employees and to move forward with recreating the PwC work culture so that people would feel more fully themselves, these fears had to be faced and the ColorBrave conversations were held *even as these fears were still present.* And the results were not all rainbows and butterflies—but the results from these conversations were important and honest and allowed PwC to begin taking some important steps forward.

4. Deconstruct: eliminate subjective processes.

The data that Tim Ryan got from the emails and from the ColorBrave conversations confirmed that the typical culture at PwC discouraged open conversation around race and consequently prevented minority employees from fully being themselves at work. The subjective processes in this case—employees relating to one another in a "business-as-usual" fashion—needed disruption in order to confront the biases that the minority employees were facing.

Opening up space for conversation was a vulnerable act and seemed foolish to some in leadership. There were concerns that it would appear opportunistic, or that a social media debacle would ensue,[22] but this is the work of erasing institutional bias!

5. Reconstruct with objectivity.

These smaller meeting spaces were constructed with privacy, informality, honesty, and authenticity in mind. But because there was now a dedicated space set aside for conversation, black and minority employees felt able to share, and white employees listened and many were extremely surprised. When the status quo was changed and a space was recreated with more equity in mind, people were more able to be themselves.

Employees reported that there's been a subtle shift, a willingness to listen. One associate said, "I used to think that I should treat people the way I want to be treated . . . but, really, I need to treat people the way *they* want to be treated."[23]

6. Build accountability.

While much work happened in these ground-level conversations, Tim Ryan's vision for PwC is for there to be an overall change at institutional levels. Because we spend a good portion of our time at work, and because we are our best selves when we can be our most authentic selves, Tim Ryan sees these conversations as potential for greater world change. Ryan has asked that all of PwC's units continue to hold the ColorBrave conversations regularly, as a discipline of communication and as an accountability measure.

Ryan is leading the charge in gathering other Fortune 500 CEOs to work together on even more difficult issues of race. While the gathering hasn't shared yet what it plans to do, over two dozen CEOs who have signed on, and the group is a rather unconventional list which includes competitors of PwC.

Racial Bias in Housing

Racial bias in housing is such a pervasive issue that there are equal housing opportunity laws in the United States and many organizations dedicated to the surfacing and enforcement of discriminatory housing practices. Housing Opportunities Made Equal (HOME) is a national organization headquartered in Richmond, Virginia. Helen O'Beirne Hardiman served as their Director of Fair Housing for three years and is currently the Vice President of

Law and Policy at HOME. She shared the following thoughts on institutional bias:

> *I see racism, sexism, and ableism in how nonprofits are structured so hierarchically. Men tend to make more money than women, white people tend to be in leadership more than people of color, and interns of color are too often ignored while working hard for no pay. The topics of mental and physical disabilities are taboo in the workplace. Enduring cultures of nonconfrontation ensure these institutional biases persist.*
>
> *I am angry that institutional bias pervades nonprofits because we work at organizations that stand for justice and equality. The hypocrisy is frustrating. I am also saddened to realize that I am a part of this institutional bias and as a white person, I benefit from it.*
>
> *I have not been able to change the status quo which feels like a force more powerful than gravity! In places where I can make a difference, I am intentional about recognizing institutional bias and working against it, like not requiring a college degree for employment opportunities and making sure we recruit a pool of candidates that includes people of color and people with disabilities.*

Danny Hicks, a Virginia based realtor, shared the following:

> *Bias has been such a common practice in real estate that it has been named and outlawed by fair housing laws dating all the way back to 1968 and then amended in 1988 and 1991. Questions about these laws show up on every real estate licensure exam I have ever taken. I would be lying if I said that I had*

never been told by a landlord or seller who I was representing what race preference they would have for the tenant or buyers.

I am usually able to counsel them that such a request is illegal, unethical, and financially foolish, but on one such occasion where the seller insisted, I was forced to walk away from the listing altogether. I am not the only agent who has experienced this. My broker tells the following story when training new agents.

One evening he listed a home for sale for a young couple who were also wanting to upgrade to a larger home. The listed home was in great shape, well-kept, and would have sold easily. Upon returning the next day to take photos, one owner pulled him aside, and stated, "Just so you know, we do not want you to show the home to any black buyers." Being somewhat curt, the broker stated, "No problem. I will not be showing the home to any buyers, as I can no longer represent you under this directive. What you are asking me to do is illegal and immoral."

Of course, with the release (loss) of the listing, the broker also lost out on the homeowners' next home purchase. This stand against discrimination cost him nearly $8,000 in net commissions, but not at the expense of his reputation.

When TMI Consulting project managed the "Race: Are We So Different?" traveling exhibit for the Science Museum of Virginia, we facilitated dozens of dialogues for work teams. The purpose of the exhibit was to highlight how the social construct of race has affected people around the world over time. The most important takeaway from the exhibit is that the whole concept of race was created by people to subjugate people of color.

The notions of tribal affiliation and genetic ancestry have always been part of the human experience. National affiliation entered the picture after humans created the social construct of nations by drawing lines on maps and naming the spaces between them. But racial classifications were developed to support the justification of the transatlantic slave trade by otherwise morally upright Christians. The only way good, God-fearing people could sleep at night while they stole, raped, murdered, and obliterated people and nations was to make themselves believe that the victims of their oppression were somehow less than human.

Let's all take a moment and think back to grade school science class. In 1735, Carl Linnaeus, a Swedish scientist, published *Systema Naturae* which introduced the idea of a new way to look at taxonomy and animal nomenclature. Like most modern textbooks, it went through several new editions and in 1758, the tenth, and arguably most important, edition was published.

This tenth edition saw Linnaeus break down the animal kingdom into six classes, with class one being Mammalia, or mammal. From there, Linnaeus further categorized things until he got to the genus *Homo*, meaning "human being" or "man." This is the narrative that we grew up hearing, but what may not be as well known is that Linnaeus went on to propose five *taxa* or categories: *Americanus*, *Asiaticus*, *Africanus*, *Europeanus*, and *Monstrosus*.

While it is not hard to interpret where Linnaeus geographically categorized the first four, the fifth has been a source of debate. Some argue that the fifth category, *Monstrosus*, serves as a miscellanea category while others argue that this is the category where he placed those with visible disabilities.

As genealogy has advanced over the past several centuries, we have learned the truth: all of modern humankind can trace its lineage back to Africa. We lived there, evolved there, and through migrations occurring between 120,000 and 50,000 years ago, Homo sapiens spread across the globe. [23]

Presumably because Linnaeus was a white European, he categorized white people (Americanus and Europeanus) as superior to the black (Africanus), Asian (Asiaticus), and disabled (Monstrosus) classifications. The problem with Linnaeus' hierarchical system is that it continues to affect people to this day, despite the fact that most of us know that there is no such thing as a lesser human. The hierarchy of human value is one of the most effective and pernicious fallacies ever created. So many systems and institutions were built on a foundation of this concept. It is at the very root of the institutional bias problem. If we could obliterate the belief that some people are innately more valuable than others, we would quickly see the end of systemic bias as there would cease to be a reason to protect the imbalance.

The "Race: Are We So Different?" exhibit features a section on housing discrimination. During one of the workgroup dialogues, an African American gentleman shared the following story:

> *I was in the process of selling my house, so I hired an appraiser to assess the value of my property. The appraiser gave us a quote that was significantly lower than my neighbors' houses. I knew the approximate value of the property, so I hired another appraiser and the value was still way too low. The two appraisals were $15,000 to $30,000 under value.*
>
> *I brought a real estate agent who was a friend over to look at the house and he told me that we would need to get rid of all of the art and images that indicated a black family lived in the house. I was*

dumbfounded. After the implications of his statement sunk in, I took his advice. The next appraiser came and valued the house within the range I had originally expected—with no evidence of African American residents visible.

It is important for people to realize that these things are still happening in contemporary societies despite the presence of rules and laws opposing such biased and discriminatory behavior. Obviously, if you are part of a real-estate agency or network that you recognize is engaging in this type of behavior, it is imperative that you take steps to break the cycle. In this case, the institutional bias is illegal in the United States.

Are you willing to lose money to do the right thing like Danny Hicks and his agents, or are you willing to support the status quo and harm thousands of innocent families whose only crime is being born into a marginalized demographic?

Inaction and silence are choices. Sometimes your silence harms people. More of us need to choose to follow the six steps and break down institutional bias before it causes more harm.

Chapter Six

Hiring/Advancement
Bias

One of the most common complaints we hear from organizational leaders seeking to increase diversity and inclusion is that there aren't enough diverse, qualified candidates. We never want to seem condescending, but there are plenty of people of all races and ethnicities and all educational and experience levels seeking employment.

There is a privilege that comes with representing an institution. We expect candidates to find us. After all, we are offering jobs. And the candidates with access and exposure will find us. Unfortunately, that often means people who are connected and networked within the same systems as the institution and its existing workforce will find us. In many situations, even if diverse, qualified staff, are in the workforce, they don't seem to be promoted into leadership positions.

Hiring/advancement bias presents itself in a multitude of ways:

- Homogeneous workforce
- Diversity concentrated at the lowest levels of the organization
- Homogeneous applicants
- Lack of visible diversity in leadership
- Lack of diversity recruitment/retention strategy
- Lack of concern about diversity
- Failure to invest in mentoring, professional development, and succession planning
- Failure to cast a wide recruiting net

- Disqualification of candidates based on ethnic names
- Disqualification of candidates based on social media photos
- Disqualification of candidates based on accents/dialects
- Disqualification of candidates based on anything that is not related to the job duties
- Disqualification of candidates because they aren't a "culture fit"

These are just a few of the many ways hiring bias can present itself. Let's take a closer look at them.

Homogeneous Workforce

We encounter a lot of workplaces that have become homogeneous. This is often the result of relying too heavily on employee referrals, employee networks, alma maters, and so on. A workplace is still homogeneous if its 100 percent minority owned and operated, so this isn't just a white thing. If only one race, gender, or other demographic is represented, it's homogeneous and poses a business risk. Companies with diverse employee populations and diverse leadership are more profitable, innovative, and resilient.

You have to remember that a candidate who does not see diversity represented at your organization has no way of knowing whether it happened by design or by default. The United States, in particular, is not that many decades removed from legally banning minority groups from the workplace. In fact, some minority groups can *still* be legally excluded from the workplace in many states. The state of Virginia, for instance, allows employers to terminate sexual minorities or not hire them because they identify as LGBTQIA, so there are still workplaces that would rather not be bothered with diversity.

Even when forces mandate inclusion, the attitude of intolerance creates an air of hostility that bedevils minorities in ways that cause undue stress, anxiety, and disillusionment. No one wants to work in under such conditions. It is therefore very important that your organization be authentic in its understanding whether its homogeneous workforce is deliberate or accidental. Once you determine that there is bias in your workplace, whether accidental or deliberate, you have a responsibility to rectify the situation

Diversity Concentrated at the Lowest Levels of the Organization

Some companies are able to hire diverse, qualified staff, but only for entry-level assignments. In this case, leaders need to be charting paths for lower-level employees to advance and be promoted over time. Diversity concentrated at the bottom is a detractor for diverse high-potential candidates. If people do not see reflections of themselves in leadership, they are apt to believe that the job you are posting is a dead-end career move.

Diversity at the entry level is not inherently problematic. However, experiencing diversity concentrated at the bottom of the organizational chart as sufficiently representative is not a very inclusive outlook. If your organization is not actively asking why the organization is segregated by employment classification, then you do have an issue that raises concerns. We do not wish to be the bearers of bad news, but pretending something is okay in the face of clear evidence of institutional bias is not socially responsible.

None of us wants to believe that we are part of the problem. Nonetheless, if you have any degree of leadership, management, administrative, hiring, or other instrumental influence within an organizational and you do nothing to address these issues, *you are part of the problem*. It really is as simple as that. It is not anyone else's job to fix it. It is your job to see the problem, investigate it, evaluate your role in perpetuating the bias, define your new role in erasing the bias, and cultivate allies before pursuing the six steps to erase it once and for all.

Homogeneous Applicants/Homogeneous Leadership

People frequently tell us they aren't getting enough demographic representation during the recruitment phase. It is not enough to say something, you must do something. Cast a wider net. Go where the people are. If your organization or leadership is homogeneous, diverse applicants have no way of knowing whether this is by default or by design.

It is your organization's responsibility to show up where people are and put out a welcome mat. Visit different colleges and universities, professional association for various ethnicities and demographics, and expand your network to include new people in new places.

Scanning to expand is one way to grow your network. Some of you may remember the chapter called "Scan to Expand" in *Overcoming Bias.* When it comes to scanning to expand, notions such as being colorblind or gender-neutral need to be put aside, as does any interpretation of a comfort zone.

Consider your circle or in-group: what does that demographic look like? What are their political views? If the mental diversity inventory you're doing right now finds itself wanting, then it may be time to expand your circle. Look for ways to connect yourself to new viewpoints and new habits. These goals can be gradual and range in magnitude, but the effort and objectives remain the same. Here are some possibilities:

- Volunteer to join diverse teams and committees.
- Out yourself as a cultural ally by standing up when biased comments are made.

- Seek out the opinions of your colleagues from your out-group.

- Make suggestions that are respectful of the opinions, experiences, and perspectives of your out-groups.

- Expand the list of people you invite to work-related or after-work outings.[1]

Scanning to expand is never a one-and-done deal. It necessitates deliberate effort and ongoing, intentional choice to open up your in-group. This solution is applicable to many of the recruitment-based bias challenges.

Lack of Diversity Recruitment/Retention Strategy

Does your recruitment strategy only include posting jobs in mainstream outlets? Are you reaching out to a broad array of representative communities? Organizational recruiters often overlook minority publications, diverse media outlets, and places like historically black colleges and universities (HBCUs).

Is your slate of candidates diverse? Some organizations go so far as to refuse to proceed with an interview panel until the candidate pool is diverse. You have a 100 percent chance of failing to diversify your staff if the only people who make it to the interviews are homogeneous. And a minority candidate has no statistical chance of being hired if they are the only one. Women and racial minorities are more likely to be hired if there are at least two minority groups represented in the slate of candidates.[2]

Failure to Invest in Mentoring, Professional Development, and Succession Planning

If your organization is able to recruit and hire diverse, qualified staff, is that where your effort stops? Are you also taking steps to engage, develop, promote, and retain that same staff? Are the people being developed, engaged, and promoted all representative of one race or gender? Do people of all demographics know where they fall in the succession plan?

We recognize that these are tough questions, and sometimes the answers are even tougher. Nonetheless, if we seek to instigate change and improvement, it is imperative that we be willing to examine the facts.

Disqualification of Candidates Based on Ethnic Names

Some people are not aware that this happens, but recruiters have admitted that they disqualify candidates when their names sound ethnic. Sometimes it's black names, names that sound foreign, or names they find hard to pronounce. These recruiters often feel they are doing the organization a huge favor by keeping ethnic-sounding people out of the running. They believe that the person won't enjoy having their name constantly mispronounced, or that the foreign person might cause the organization undue stress because people might not understand their accent. The recruiters are, of course, assuming that a foreign name will be attached to an incomprehensible accent.

How people handle accents is interesting. People are often given an incredible amount of grief over their accents. In the context of our training, we frequently ask people with accents to identify themselves. Typically, a handful of people from various nations raise their hands. We then take a moment to remind everyone in the room that we *all* speak with accents, we just have a habit of being in the company of people with the same accent as our own. If you relocate anyone and drop them on the other side of their country or into another country, their accent will become very apparent to those around them.

The intent of this exercise is to help people see that ostracizing or becoming frustrated with people because of their speech patterns is short-sighted and unfair. All it takes to understand an accent is patience and practice. And we must increase our compassion toward one another to care enough to make that small but significant effort.

Disqualification of Candidates
Based on Social Media Photos

Many articles warn job seekers to be mindful of what they place on social media. Employers can find you online and if they see you behaving in a manner unbefitting an employee of their organization, well, they may move on. It is certainly not legal to disqualify based on the categories that are protected in your organization, city, state, or nation. And protected catagories do vary from nation to nation and state to state. But it is legal, in the United States for instance, to use social media as an extension of a resume to ascertain the sincerity, credibility, and professionalism of a candidate.

The problem with social media screening is that humans are inherently biased and they may take action beyond what is legal. Again, this may not always be intentional, but it can become a form of institutional bias if left unchecked, and if it results in the screening out of some demographics and not others.

Candidate "Culture Fit"

When an organization achieves enough success that they are in a position to increase their workforce, they sometimes attribute part or all of their success to the existing workplace culture. The existing culture may very well be a major reason for their success. Unfortunately, organizational culture fit is not a great way to weed out candidates. Diversity of thought, education, perspective, and countless other variables have been proven to increase profitability, group intelligence, and efficacy in organizations. Nonetheless, hiring managers have been known to reject applicants on the basis of culture fit.

People from diverse demographics lose job opportunities as a result of being a poor culture fit— meaning "they won't fit in." This unoriginal excuse for supporting hegemony, or the predominant culture, is an admission that an organizational culture is weak, fragile, and unsupportive of people.

A Princeton University meta-analysis indicated that there has been no change in the rates of hiring discrimination against African Americans between 1990 and 2015. Explicit racism has declined, but the subtle forms of bias have not changed over time.[3]

In the case of hiring bias, anyone in the organization, including you, can own the responsibility of identifying the bias at play. Someone must call the bias out and name it for what it is. Once you and your allies agree on the bias operating within a given system, it's time to (1) **set a clear intention**.

- We have a hiring bias and we want to eliminate it.

How do you know you have a hiring bias? Can you prove it? If you can substantiate the claim and confirm it with data, you may be able to attract more allies and get traction for subsequent action. Gather all of the data you can to prove your hypothesis. Always (2) **lead with data** as it is more effective than relying solely on emotional appeals. Leverage your allies to use their connections and resources as force multipliers to expedite this process and every other step along the way.

- Data indicate that our staff is largely homogeneous. Most of our staff share a socioeconomic class, race, and educational status.

Be thorough in your data gathering. Are you looking at coincidences or patterns that bear out the same results? An (3)

accurate diagnosis will help sustain the effort and facilitate overcoming objections.

- We hire our employees from the same recruiting sources. Our candidate pool is also homogeneous. We actually *want* diversity but we never achieve it.

Once you are confident that you have sufficient data to support an accurate diagnosis and your intention to eliminate a specific system bias is clear, it's time to (4) **deconstruct**. **Eliminating subjective processes** helps ferret out biases that have become embedded within systems.

- We are removing limiting constructs from the hiring process including "culture fit," "shared interests," and "appearance."

After systems have been successfully deconstructed and subjective bias rooted out, then it is time to rebuild. (5) **Reconstructing with objectivity** introduces transparency and accountability for the maintenance of unbiased systems. Berrett-Koehler Publishers modeled this step with the following "Individual Performance Standards" that were created to decrease bias in hiring and increase diversity in the organization.

- *Applicant's track record of proactively taking initiative to institute innovations and advances that addressed needs, solved problems, and exploited opportunities*

- *Applicant's history of performing responsibilities with accuracy, completeness, timeliness, and efficiency*

- *Applicant's history of making themselves accountable for performance and delivering on their accountabilities*

- *Applicant's history of continually advancing their own learning and development*

- *Applicant's history of maintaining a positive, engaged, committed attitude, even in a challenging environment*

- *Applicant's history of collaborating well with coworkers and being a supportive and responsible citizen in previous organizational settings*

The final step is to (6) **build in accountability and ongoing measurement**. New systems need clear accountability and success metrics to support sustainability. If the system updates are measured, progress can be documented and recalibrated as needed. Accountability ensures that all parties with access to system inputs continue to maintain the integrity of the intended changes.

- *We will empower a hiring review team to ensure the bias-prevention steps are implemented. Failure to adhere to the hiring protocol will result in immediate corrective action. The team will continue to monitor and measure progress from the original baseline toward any stated goals.*

Wishing and hoping for changes in hiring and advancement bias, as with other institutional bias, is insufficient for disrupting the status quo. Clear, organized, decisive action is required. The six steps can be instrumental in aiding you as you begin the journey of erasing systemic bias.

If you have read this far, then you are likely aware of at least one bias that may be plaguing your organization. That is assuming you did not already know what the issue was before you picked up this book. At this point, you should see a clear pattern for addressing your specific institutional bias using the six-step formula.

There is a tremendous power in naming the problem. There is even more power in quantifying the problem and supporting your hypothesis with metrics. Approaching the issues of institutional bias with the surgical precision of a scientist in search of measurable solutions is a sure way to garner support from like-minded people.

The bottom line is that most people believe that they are inherently good. While there is a minority of people who are cruel and proud of it, we believe that humanity is largely made up of decent people who are doing their best, or at the very least, trying to do their best. It is one thing to meander through one's work life without seeing, naming, or consciously acknowledging the disparities and injustices that simmer beneath the surface of an organizational culture. It is another thing entirely to be shown the subtle discriminatory behaviors or consequences affecting actual human beings in your proximity.

If you succeed in making a strong enough case using the four preparatory steps, what you reveal to your colleagues can usually not be unseen. Turning a blind eye to the problem once it has been named and enumerated is just cruel. And, again, you have to do the hard work of figuring out who will be threatened by the revelation of injustice. Answering the discernment questions in chapter 2 in advance of your cultivating allies is critical.

Chapter Seven

Customer Bias

Retail

The first thing that comes to mind when we think of customer bias is the allegory of the car salesman. In the story, two people walk onto a car lot. One of the people is impeccably dressed and the other looks disheveled at best. The two car salespeople on the lot flip a coin for first choice at a customer. The salesperson who wins is ecstatic as he approaches the well-dressed patron.

We think you know how this story ends. Turns out the well-dressed customer doesn't buy anything and instead spends an hour and a half of the salesperson's time asking questions and test-driving fancy cars. The disheveled customer, on the other hand, was wealthy and decisive. She knew what she wanted and came prepared to purchase. It's a "don't judge a book by its cover" story, but it happens all the time. The winner of the coin toss was biased against the poorly dressed customer and lost a sale as a result. Did you assume the patrons were male even though women are statistically more likely to make major household purchasing decisions? How many businesses miss opportunities and lose customers because of bias?

Nonprofits

Customer bias is not a phenomenon that is exclusive to the for-profit economic sector. We have also worked with nonprofit organizations that recognized they were missing out on potential donors due to inadvertent donor profiling. When you think of a large nonprofit organization, who do you picture as the people who can afford to make donations?

If you reread that last sentence, even the question was laced with customer bias. Who are we to judge who *can afford* to donate if we don't have access to people's finances and spending habits? Are we prejudging donors based on occupation, socioeconomic status, age, or some other external variable that we think we can ascertain? All of this is problematic because wealthy, older, white people are a commonly sought-after donor demographic.

Nonprofits are increasingly seeing the value in nurturing relationships with younger, middle-class donors of all races. Most importantly, the truly forward-thinking nonprofits are building authentic relationships with people who have far less disposable income than average, sometimes meeting them through their service offerings, and sometimes through community engagement.

It turns out that if you cultivate honest relationships with people while they don't have a lot to offer you, they can (1) remember the impact your organization had in their lives once they get to the other side of their struggle or (2) find ways to shape the vision and clarity of an organization's mission and vision that far exceed financial donations, empowering an organization to empower those in need despite whatever made them not fit the profile of a typical donor.

Performing Arts

Another example of customer bias takes place frequently in the performing arts. Theatre, television, and film producers, for instance, have habitually cast majority demographics to all or most roles in their productions.

One of the most egregious approaches to this was the use of blackface—a practice of painting white people to depict other races when they could have hired actors of color. This shameless practice began with staged minstrel shows in the late 1800s yet continued all the way through to the early film era with well-known actors such as Bing Crosby and Buster Keaton performing in blackface on film. This practice was mostly eliminated by the 1930s but still made appearances in cartoons and some film through the 1960s, when the Civil Rights movement helped push this practice to an end.

Unfortunately, a similar bias takes the form of "whitewashing" in modern film and television. The 2015 film *Aloha* features a nearly all-white cast yet is set in the state of Hawaii. One of the characters, Allison Ng, is stated to have parents of Chinese and Native Hawaiian descent, yet the character is portrayed by Emma Stone, a Caucasian actress.[1]

The Academy of Motion Picture Arts and Sciences annually nominates films, actors, and associated professionals for the Oscars, also known as the Academy Awards. In 2016, there was a public backlash against the Academy for failing to nominate any minority actors or majority-minority–cast films for the Oscars. A hashtag was developed, #OscarsSoWhite, and a boycott ensued.

In April 2012, acclaimed television producer Shonda Rhimes debuted a TV show called *Scandal* starring Kerry Washington. Shonda Rhimes is the award-winning screenwriter and executive producer of *Grey's Anatomy*. What was remarkable about *Scandal* was that it was the first prime time American TV show starring an African American woman since 1970. The common assumption was that none of the major networks believed an African American woman could carry a show, or more likely, that no one would tune in. The doubt aimed at Rhimes and Kerry Washington at the launch of *Scandal* is clear customer bias, and is epidemic in Hollywood's entertainment industry.

In fact, this kind of customer bias in Hollywood is so epidemic that the Bunche Center for African American Studies at UCLA has begun regularly releasing a report on Hollywood's diversity problem. Their report discovered that much of the problem happens because the position from which "green light-ing" decisions are made in the Hollywood industry are over-whelmingly dominated by white males—and the perception, conscious or unconscious—is that the television and movie indus-tries are best propped up by white males.

Even in "diverse" broadcast television, white actors were found to monopolize the top credits, and racial and gender stereotypes, though muted, were still present in virtually all shows. LGBT char-acters were almost always relegated to lower-credited actors. Across the board, minority leads were more prominent in only sitcoms, while white leads were featured in both sitcoms and dramas.[2]

Despite these findings, the Hollywood Diversity Report also named something that most of us already know—this institu-tional bias not only creates inequity, but it's also based on mis-guided assumptions on the part of television and film executives. Films with diverse casts made the most money at the box office and cashed in on their investments with the most success.

Median viewer ratings were highest for broadcast and cable scripted shows written by minorities and these same ratings peaked for shows with diverse casts. In other words, not only is Hollywood's customer bias wrong—it's costing Hollywood view-ers and money!

Let's look back at *Scandal* for a moment. Remember the net-work's assumption that an African American woman couldn't carry a dramatic television series and that no one would tune in? Well, both theories were proven wrong as millions of viewers tuned in and as of 2018 it was ranked TV's fastest-growing return-ing series. *Scandal* is one of the most popular shows on social media and has been acknowledged by many of the major televi-sion awards.

In 2018, Marvel Studios and Disney Motion Pictures released *Black Panther*, a superhero movie with a predominantly black cast. It quickly became the highest grossing film by a black director, despite Hollywood's ongoing reluctance to feature a majority minority cast for fear of box office failure. As of the writing of this book, *Black Panther* is also the ninth highest grossing movie of all time.

It may be obvious that the minority actors who are not often cast in lead roles might be disheartened by the bias present at all levels in the performing arts. What many people may *not* know is that the majority white and male actors who are cast can be just as disillusioned by bias in the arts. Seasoned actor Scott Wichman shared the following perspective:

> *Since childhood, the protagonists of virtually every major story's narrative have been white. It caused me to view myself as "The Hero of the Story" in a visceral way while growing up. I saw people who looked like me, who were the "heroes of the story" and I was filled with an intrinsic confidence that the world was "made for me."*
>
> *That is an invaluable mindset for a child to have— to be able to look at popular culture and absorb the message that "You're the hero of the story." It is really tough to imagine what my life would have been like without that ever-present influence while growing up. Whether it was Luke Skywalker or Superman, I have always seen people who looked like me doing amazing things on screen.*
>
> *And, in my career, I have also benefited from lead roles in stories about white people while never really stopping to think about the implications of that.*

When asked whether he has been able to change the status quo, Mr. Wichman responded:

I am part of the status quo in my community. I feel that it is up to me to listen and advocate for a shift in the stories we tell and the representation of individuals in the stories we choose to tell.

Technology

By now we are certain that you have figured out the pattern. Never underestimate the power of any demographic to exceed your expectations as customers. Product developers have long known that one cannot predict precisely how a product will be used or be received by customers.

There are countless innovations that have emerged due to customer exposure, so limiting your customer base limits creativity and growth.

The Nintendo Wii, for instance, was a phenomenal innovation in gaming as it allowed users to stand up and exercise their bodies while interacting with videogames. Nintendo is a gaming platform that has historically been marketed to children and young adults. Well, it turned out that when the Wii hit the market, it was immensely popular with senior citizens. Wii was not marketing directly toward the older demographic, but seniors were using the tech to get out of their chairs, get moving, and enjoy themselves. Nintendo executives ultimately decided to actively market to seniors and created an entirely new market share for the company.[3]

Food and Beverage

In the United States, there is a widely held perception among restaurant servers that black people do not tip as generously as white people.[4] One could argue that the massive and ever-widening income disparity between races in the USA likely contributes to said phenomenon because black people have far less disposable income than white people on average.[5] Nonetheless, perception tends to influence reality, and the problem with that is that it perpetuates a vicious cycle.

When restaurant staff expect smaller tips from black customers, they may deliberately or inadvertently provide subpar service. If you were a black customer, or a customer of any race, would you be inclined to offer a generous tip for bad service? So the cycle continues. When you add to this the historical legacy of humiliating treatment of African Americans in restaurants before, during, and for a while after the Civil Rights movement, this bias only adds salt to the wounds of those who still remember those days.

What Do We Do?

It is important that as we scan our institutions for possible biases, we do not omit the customer experience. We definitely want you to take plenty of time to consider the needs and experiences of employees within the workforce, but not to the exclusion of, or at the expense of, your customers. Institutional bias can affect any of your stakeholders, so taking a comprehensive scan is very important.

EXERCISE 6

Guidelines for Customer Bias Review

1. Do you have a clear picture of profile of the majority of your current clients?
2. How was that profile determined?
3. Who are the outliers?
4. Could the outlier client demographics be expanded?
5. Who is not a client demographic?
6. Why are they not clients? (Do you not want them as clients? If not, there's likely a bias in the mix.)

---

7. How could you expand your client base to include the missing demographics?

8. Do your competitors have the clients you are not reaching?

9. Do you have a way to survey or poll your customers and potential customers?

Once you have asked yourself and key stakeholders in your organization the aforementioned questions, then you should review the preliminary four steps before embarking on the six steps to erase your customer bias. In review, the four steps from Exercise 1, Preliminary Personal Work, Individual Focus, are:

1. Evaluate your (old) role in perpetuating systemic bias.

2. Define your (new) role in breaking down systemic bias.

3. Cultivate allies.

4. Create a movement.

The six steps to erase institutional bias include:

1. Set a clear intention.

2. Lead with data.

3. Diagnose accurately.

4. Deconstruct: eliminate subjective processes.

5. Reconstruct with objectivity.

6. Build in accountability and ongoing measurement.

Chapter Eight

Retribution Bias

So far, we have tackled a number of biases that work in a number of dangerous ways. In these final two chapters, we are turning toward a bias that enacts oppression by tapping into intersecting unconscious biases of race, class, and gender and adding in a particularly American notion of retributive justice, which not only harms people within organizations but functionally keeps people out of our workplaces and organizations. This bias is "retribution bias."

We're going to be spending the next two chapters on retribution bias because it has such a tremendous impact on people's lives—economically, socially, and spiritually. If we think of institutional biases as social forces, this particular bias has acted in powerful and oppressive ways to harm millions of people.

We define "retribution bias" as a socially held and institutionally enacted bias toward exacting retribution—a bias favoring punishment. Retribution bias is triggered in the presence of wrongdoing, or the perception of wrongdoing, and depends, in the American context, on the criminal justice system to name who is trustworthy, hirable, a "safe community member," and so on. Retribution bias replaces the restorative instinct to develop, maintain, or (re)build relationship. Restoring relationship can be between the offender and offended, or between the perceived offender and his or her full relationship with community—in other words, restoring citizenship with all its rights, freedoms, and responsibilities.

What makes retribution bias complex and powerful is the intersection of oppressions by which it is funded. Retribution bias relies squarely on the unconscious biases that many of us hold against people who have contact with the criminal justice system; the often-biased way that the criminal justice system carries out its tasks by implicating the poor, people of color, and gender minorities at disproportionate rates; and the lack of real proportionate relationship between crime and punishment. For example, mandatory minimums, instituted by the Boggs Act of 1951, eventually grew to bind judges by law to sentence offenders to longer and longer sentences for nonviolent drug crimes. And a shocking report issued in 2013 by the American Civil Liberties Union (ACLU) found that about 79 percent of 3,278 prisoners serving life without parole were sentenced to die in prison for nonviolent crimes. A list of these crimes compiled by the ACLU included acting as a go-between in the sale of $10 of marijuana to an undercover officer, having a trace amount of cocaine in clothes pockets so minute it was invisible to the naked eye and detected only in lab tests, and—horrifyingly—having a stash of over-the-counter decongestant pills that could be manufactured into methamphetamine.[1]

The overwhelming majority—83.4 percent—of the life-without-parole sentences for nonviolent crimes surveyed by the ACLU were mandatory. In these cases, the sentencing judges were bound by law to enact sentencing due to required mandatory minimum periods of imprisonment, habitual offender laws, statutory penalty enhancements, or other sentencing rules that mandated life without parole. Charging decisions—which determine whether defendants will face charges that automatically trigger mandatory minimums—are made by federal and state prosecutors, who, data has shown, are often (not always, of course) motivated by public opinions about safety and personal political gain.[2]

When compared to other nations, the American picture of the relationship between crime and punishment is distinct. As long ago as the 1980s when, according to an analysis by David

Farrington of Cambridge University and Patrick Langan of the US Bureau of Justice Statistics, the likelihood of someone found guilty of burglary going behind bars was 40 percent in England and Wales but 74 percent in the United States.[3] The difference is even greater now.

When it comes to robbery crimes, which are often classified as violent, the picture is complex, as well. In the mid-1980s, the United States was about as likely to imprison convicted robbers as England but considerably more likely to do so than West Germany. This has increased with higher penalties for robbery crimes.[4] The American version of retribution bias has a vast and storied history that will help you understand how this, and many other biases, can have extremely deep and connected roots.

Understanding the depth of a bias's origins can help you comprehend what you are contending with as you strive to erase the systemic biases you encounter. Taking the time to learn the history of a bias will strengthen your resolve and your ability to take a well-informed stand in the face of injustice.

The American justice system has historically been heavily focused toward punitive measures of addressing crime. The United States has also nurtured a culture of retribution bias that was born out of an impulse to protect the livelihood of only a small portion of people (namely white men).

When it comes to specifics in the criminal justice system, retribution bias manifests itself now in public support for criminal justice policies that inflict punishment for violations of laws and skew heavily toward exacting this punishment on minority communities.

Because of the racial history of the United States and the power of increasingly retributive policies, the justice system in general has a significantly greater impact on the poor and communities of color. Punishment means that those who were originally excluded from the declaration of independence, because they were not seen as fully human, are now excluded from full citizenship as they are branded criminals and felons. They are stripped of their basic civil and human rights, such as welfare rights, the right to vote, the right to be free of legal discrimination in employment and housing, the right to education, and the right to serve on juries.

The Impact of Retribution Bias

This may seem like a more unfamiliar bias and one that is pretty far removed from your workplace or organization. The uncomfortable reality is that this particular bias—retribution bias—has a reach that means all of us are implicated and impacted. So, if you're wondering whether or not it affects people in your organization, it does.

Retribution bias can impact us directly when we or our loved ones have to navigate the penal system. Such an event gives us a sickening familiarity with the manner in which this bias exacts control and restricts lives. It can impact us by distancing us from full relationship with people in the world. Put more simply, there are untold numbers of people missing from workplaces, organizations, and lives because of retribution bias.

Retribution bias—the bias favoring punishment—is built squarely on a foundation of racial and ethnic biases. When the Sentencing Project did its pioneering study on racial perceptions of crime and support for punitive policies,[5] published in 2014, one of their more staggering findings was the depth and complexity of implicit and explicit associations between crime and race or ethnicity. In their research, they found that even individuals who "explicitly disavowed prejudice" had implicit bias when it came to criminal stereotypes. The researchers also found that these stereotypes corresponded directly to their support for harsher and more violent policing and more punitive measures.

In a supporting study that Sentencing Project researchers examined, subjects used video simulations. They were asked to quickly identify and shoot armed subjects, but not shoot unarmed subjects. This study found that nonblack participants more quickly and accurately shot at armed black, Latino, and Asian targets than armed white targets.[6]

This association between African Americans and Latinos and crime moves beyond just individuals and shapes general impressions of neighborhoods as well. Researchers determined that, again, even amongst those who strongly disavowed racism, people who live in neighborhoods with a higher proportion of racial minorities are more likely to actually overestimate crime rates. Even after accounting for a number of measures of disorder, they found that, "the percentage of young black men is one of the best predictors of the perceived severity of neighborhood crime."[7] **Their conclusion: the race and ethnicity of the "other" significantly distorts people's perception of risk.**

America has seen this in the increased media exposure of the tragic shooting deaths of Philando Castile, Oscar Grant, Renisha McBride, Trayvon Martin, and Stephon Clark. Thus, when people—both those in law enforcement and those who look to law enforcement for protection—believe that there is a greater risk, they will look to harsher and more punitive measures to be held up in the criminal justice system.

This has proved to be true. Americans' support for punitive measures—the strength of our retribution bias—falls largely along racial lines. In the Sentencing Project's introduction to their study, they describe their conclusions about the misconceptions and impact of retribution bias.

White Americans, who constitute a majority of policy-makers, criminal justice practitioners, the media, and the general public, overestimate the proportion of crime committed by people of color and the proportion of racial minorities who commit crime. Even individuals who denounce racism often harbor unconscious and unintentional racial biases.

Attributing crime to racial minorities limits empathy toward offenders and encourages retribution as the primary response to crime. Consequently, although whites experience less crime than people of color, they are more punitive. . . . Whites' associations of crime with people of color have helped to make the criminal justice system more punitive toward people of all races, and especially toward racial minorities, through several mechanisms.

First, the public's racial perceptions of crime have gone hand-in-hand with its support for punitive crime policy, to which elected officials, prosecutors, and judges have been responsive. Second, these perceptions directly influence the work of criminal justice practitioners and policymakers, who are not immune to these widely held biases.[8]

Retribution bias capitalizes on our unconscious biases and inserts strong language of criminalization to justify and perpetuate America's violent and oppressive practices toward people of color. America has the highest incarceration rate in the world, and one in nine US prisoners are serving life sentences. Even more astonishingly, the United States is the only western democracy still using the death penalty.[9]

While public feelings about crime and punishment—particularly among white Americans—can masquerade as fair and appropriate, retribution in the United States has always been severe and selectively aimed at black, brown, and poor bodies. Retribution bias endorses a justice system that has acted as a control mechanism, keeping minority communities disadvantaged and subjugated rather than actually impacting crime rates.

A Brief History

One might believe that American bias toward retribution has backfired, creating an oppressive monstrosity. However, it has actually benefited the interests of controlling parties throughout American history and continues to do so today.

To truly understand the fuel behind American retribution bias, you have to start at the birth of America. There are a number of events and decisions that should be understood to get a full picture of how deeply embedded slavery is to its national identity. We'll just say, for now, that at the United States' inception, the founding fathers were advancing radical new ideas of not only freedom and citizenship but also race. These ideas grew in direct connection with one another.

At the end of the eighteenth century, our infant nation was beginning to live underneath the idea that "all men are created equal." Simultaneously, the United States was significantly economically sustained by the free-labor force of enslaved Africans—the amount has been estimated to be the equivalent of trillions of dollars in modern day currency. Thus, one can see the tremendous economic pressure at play: How would this new nation hold to its ideals of human equality while enslaving large groups of people? How would the nation survive if it suddenly lost an enormous source of free labor?

If those enslaved Africans were, in fact, collectively inferior in their humanity, then they, like women and children of that age, did not have to be counted under the Declaration of Independence. The United States could both proclaim these radical ideas of equality and freedom and continue to be sustained by forced labor. In fact, Thomas Jefferson, in his *Notes on the State of Virginia*, is credited with the earliest pronouncement that, "blacks whether originally a distinct race, or made distinct by time and circumstances, are inferior to the whites in the endowments both of body and mind."[10] He wrote this in 1781, only four years after the signing the Declaration of Independence.[11]

After the Civil War, though, slavery was ostensibly abolished through the ratification of the Thirteenth Amendment, which was the first of the three Reconstruction amendments. It was passed in January of 1865 and ratified in December of that same year and says, "Neither slavery nor involuntary servitude, except as a punishment for crime whereof the party shall have been duly convicted, shall exist within the United States, or any place subject to their jurisdiction."

While it sounds wonderful that written into law is the abolition of slavery, the clause "except as a punishment for crime" moved racialized oppression from "plantation to prison."[12] There were enormous economic pressures on newly freed blacks as they tried to survive in a culture that despised their very existence, and Jim Crow laws were rapidly put into place to constrain their movement in society. In fact, the origin of the current US police system lies in the remnants of slave patrols and night watches formed to catch escaped enslaved Africans, and, post abolition, to capture freed blacks under the auspices of criminal behavior—criminal behavior that would not have been punished if committed by a white person.

Southern states quickly began to take advantage of the Thirteenth Amendment's incarceration loophole by arresting free blacks for unemployment, loitering, or gambling. Poor blacks were disproportionately prosecuted under codes known as the "Pig Laws," which incarcerated them for such crimes as stealing a farm animal. Such Black Codes circumscribed their existence so heavily that they included vagrancy statutes, making it a crime for them to be unemployed.[13] Though their freedom had just been handed to them, the criminal justice system threatened at almost every turn to immediately to take it back and re-enslave them in jails and prisons.

Once imprisoned, convicts were sold to private employers through the convict lease system, which took these "criminals" and exploited them for free labor. Public opinion moved from approving enslavement of African Americans because they were less than human to endorsing the incarceration of African Americans and other minorities because they were seen as dangerous.

After the end of slavery and the ratification of the Thirteenth Amendment, social control over minority people in the United States mostly happened through Jim Crow laws, racial terrorism, and racially biased law enforcement. After the Civil Rights movement began to threaten segregation in the 1950s and 1960s, though, a more organized "law and order" movement began to take shape.

According to Michelle Alexander, author of *The New Jim Crow: Mass Incarceration in the Age of Colorblindness*, a deliberate and coordinated effort was made by segregationists as they worried that they would not be able to discourage growing public distaste for the system of segregation. So, they began labeling civil rights activists engaged in nonviolent civil disobedience and protests as criminals and lawbreakers.

Segregationists used their public positions to perpetuate the belief that those who violated segregation laws, whether by accident or through nonviolent civil disobedience, were engaging in reckless behavior that threatened the proper social order. They drew on a law and order, retributive justice rhetoric to demand a crackdown on these criminals, and public opinion followed.[14]

It's important here to note that even before the War on Drugs was officially declared in 1982 by President Ronald Reagan, rhetoric and media portrayal were means for establishing a retribution bias and criminalizing the behavior of people of color for most of American history. In Eugene Jarecki's 2012 documentary *The House I Live In*, historian Richard Miller explains that American drug laws date back to the turn of the twentieth century and were crafted with the express purpose of criminalizing minorities. This process happened with the increasing media portrayal of minorities as criminals and a call for tough-on-crime policies to address their criminal behavior, capitalizing on racism and xenophobia to ramp up retribution bias.

For example, in 1907, California passed a series of laws making the use of opium illegal. Opium had been widely accepted before then, but California's move to make the drug illegal happened as thousands of Chinese immigrants, known to smoke the drug, were arriving. These new immigrants were subjected to hostility because they were known for working hard on railroad construction for little pay, and racist media had white Americans believing that Chinese men were luring white women to have sex in opium dens. Both the threat of cheap labor taking jobs and racialized rumors stoked American fears about Chinese immigrants.

Miller explains that you obviously couldn't lock people up simply for being Chinese, but you could lock them up and criminalize them for smoking opium, so the Anti-Opium Act was passed in 1909 by Congress. This particular law cemented

Chinese racism by making an important exception for drinking and injecting extracts of opiates, a practice that was popular among white Americans.[15]

Similarly, more states began to make cocaine illegal at the turn of the century as newspaper articles ran headlines with articles claiming, "Negro Cocaine Fiends are a New Southern Menace" and ". . . most of the attacks upon women in the South are the direct result of the cocaine-crazed Negro brain."[16] And marijuana, which was sold in pharmacies until the early part of the twentieth century, was only outlawed in the 1930s, when it became popular among Mexican-American immigrants for recreational use.

In southwest border towns, marijuana use was portrayed by both politicians and the media as causing lawlessness and turning Mexican immigrants violent, giving them superhuman strength. In 1930, Henry Aslinger was appointed the commissioner of the newly created United States Narcotics Bureau and began an aggressive national campaign that portrayed marijuana users as criminal elements, irredeemable to society.

There are countless other examples. Perhaps the most notorious and well-documented example came in 1986 when the Anti-Drug Abuse Act implemented an enormous sentencing disparity. An individual caught with one gram of crack cocaine would be subject to the same sentencing guidelines as an individual caught with 100 grams of powder cocaine. Substantial research in the intervening decades has revealed that this disparity was the result of bias, not fact. Crack cocaine is not more addictive or dangerous than powder cocaine, but was publicly associated with low-income communities of color. Public opinion was that users of crack were criminals who needed severe punishment. This statute has since been rectified by the Fair Sentencing Act of 2010, which groups are lobbying to make universally retroactive in order to address those sentenced under the old law.

The rising hysteria over crime and the need to punish criminals continued throughout the early part of the twentieth century. These concerns began to intersect and overlap with challenges to the end of segregation in the 1950s and 1960s, and all the while economic collapse was happening throughout communities of color and inner-city communities. Crime was rising, as it does during times of economic crisis, but the trifecta of economic depression for people of color, racialized ideas about criminals, and the rising enthusiasm for locking people up exploded when the War on Drugs was declared.

It's important to mention that the language of criminalization has not impacted only poor and minority communities that are largely African American, but has also driven aggressive and punitive policies toward immigrant populations. Language of criminalization and reliance on criminal prosecution (as opposed to civil enforcement and community-support programs) has significantly distorted public perception and intensified dangerous circumstances for undocumented people of all backgrounds, perhaps most notably when referencing people of Hispanic or Latino descent.

Despite language stoking fears that illegal immigrants are here to steal jobs and are dangerous, multiple studies have revealed that undocumented people are actually no more statistically likely to break laws than anyone else. On the contrary, they are more frequently criminally victimized by US citizens.[17] To put all of this more plainly, criminal justice and the criminalization of people of color has virtually always been misused as a means of control. This faulty message has been communicated to the public as "necessary" as a way to reduce crime. Retribution bias makes people believe that punishment—particularly punishment of black, brown, and poor bodies—is the catch-all way to make a safer society.

The problem is that retribution bias, like most of our biases, is based in part on misguided perceptions about the relationship between crime and incarceration. We've walked through how retribution bias has been historically popularized through the criminalization of minorities and how legal mandatory minimums increased sentences for relatively minor charges. But even if that doesn't convince you that the sentiment of retribution bias is misguided, it's important to note that there is little relationship between severity of punishment and crime deterrence. This is for several reasons, but most conclusively because of the lack of any "chastening" effect from prison sentences. Prisons may exacerbate recidivism (due, in part, to economic stressors imposed by prison at release and the fact that individuals grow out of criminal activity as they age).

In fact, our retributive system, particularly as it exploded between 1980 and 2010, did not do much to decrease crime rates but rather eroded trust between law enforcement and communities of color. Retribution bias fueled lawmakers' zeal for collateral consequences to be added to felony convictions, such as denying felons access to food stamps, federal-housing benefits, and other welfare benefits. While many states are reversing full welfare bans, the residual harm caused by releasing formerly incarcerated people back into communities without any kind of access to social or governmental safety nets has unquestionably caused harm.

Our retribution bias has not actually made our communities safer. There are multiple consequences attributed to our institutional retribution bias across the board, but greater public safety has not been one of them. The Sentencing Project concluded that the most aggravated consequences have been the following:

> *The most acute and severe consequence of these perceptions is the killing of innocent people because of racially motivated fear. A broader consequence is a criminal justice system that is on overdrive, with*

lifelong consequences for all Americans who are con-
victed of crimes, and particularly for low-income peo-
ple of color. Mass incarceration compounds economic
disadvantage, increasing the likelihood of criminal
offending across generations. The perception of a
biased criminal justice system may also foster a sense
of legal immunity among white Americans.[18]

There are still more complex and terrifying consequences for undocumented people, who often need protection, healthcare, and other services that are basic for a safe existence. Undocumented people are unable to access these resources because of the extensive and criminalizing rhetoric that has led to many of them being similarly incarcerated in subhuman conditions, because public perception is that they deserve punishment.

Retribution Bias in Perspective

Even though the United States has a significantly sized prison population, it may seem like there are many Americans—especially white Americans—who don't know anyone who has ever been locked up. Still other Americans have known many who have been in and out of jail.

Our criminal justice system has a dramatically different impact on communities of color, and while we may want to believe that we are doing better at diversity, the harsh reality is that America is still, through the lingering effects of policies and through choice, largely segregated. Brookings Institution 2015 data revealed that there have been very modest declines in segregation in the last few decades—we don't eat together, we don't socialize together, we don't worship together. The United States is more socially segregated now than it was in the height of legal, institutionalized segregation.

Because of enduring segregation, one part of the United States has positive interactions with the criminal justice system and believes it to be a well-running safeguard. Meanwhile, another part of the country has a very different experience. And this bears out in statistics. Within US borders, the numbers reveal that the criminal justice system has a dramatically different impact on lives depending on a person's race and gender.

For example, in the United States at the current incarceration rates, 5.1 percent of the population will be incarcerated in their lifetime. However, men are over eight times more likely to be locked up than women and among men—you guessed it—black men are about twice as likely as Hispanic men and six times more likely than white men to be incarcerated during their lifetime. In other words, at birth, black males have between a 1-in-3 and 1-in-4 likelihood of spending time incarcerated.

People of color account for 37 percent of the overall US population but they account for an overwhelming 67 percent of the prison population.[19] And this obviously lays the groundwork for differing perceptions about law enforcement and the criminal justice system. The Sentencing Project's 2014 report found that whites, on the whole, have fewer and more positive encounters with the police and courts relative to racial minorities, and are more likely than African Americans and Hispanics to attribute criminal behavior to individual failure rather than to contextual causes.[20]

Because of largely segregated social networks, differing rates of exposure, and qualitatively different experiences with criminal justice systems, whites tend to have higher retributive biases. White people tend to believe that law and order, tough-on-crime policies are needed to make safer communities.

It may seem logical to think that breaking the law simply deserves punishment, but even with all the historical nuances and statistics factored in, the reality is that harsher punishments and retributive justice have not worked to reduce crime. There certainly are incidents of violence and crime that offend our most humane sensibilities and demand justice. The vast majority of "crimes" in the United States can be contextualized and addressed within a better understanding of race, poverty, and our fears.

There are plenty of ways to decrease crime as it turns out! In contrast to these punitive policies are other social-policy tools, such as increased spending on education and job training, or restorative justice approaches, which are gaining traction in courtrooms across the United States. In this chapter, we have explored how our institutional bias toward retributive forms of justice is metaphorically financed by our historical racial biases. And in our next chapter, we'll look at some ways that people like you have encountered retribution bias and have worked to erase this institutional bias.

Chapter Nine

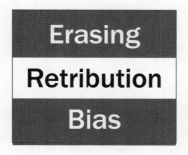

Erasing Retribution Bias

The impact of retribution bias is broad, and it can feel over-whelming to consider what it may mean to erase such an insti-tutional bias. In this chapter, we will be introducing people whose lives have intersected with this bias and we will be sharing with you how they are working to erase it. We're doing this because retribution bias tells you to steer clear of particular people.

As we explored in the last chapter, retribution bias works by consolidating many of our previously held biases and distilling them into the belief that criminals are threatening and dangerous; they're certainly not human and they're most definitely not to be a part of our organizations and workplaces. But when you get close—when you move in and encounter the people behind the mythologized images of criminals that have been held up for decades—you will find that retribution bias is not actually work-ing to keep communities safe. Retribution bias is only keeping communities fragmented and broken by inequity.

Before we look at ways that folks are working to erase this par-ticular institutional bias, we wanted to introduce you to someone who has experienced retribution bias firsthand. As we said before, retribution bias is upheld by one community while the effects and impacts are often felt over a lifetime for other communities. This is, in part, because incarceration is spread unevenly across the adult population for the reasons we addressed in the last chapter. Retri-bution bias capitalizes on racial bias, customer bias, and misin-formed pictures of who and what makes a "criminal."

Iesha Williams is in her mid-30s, works as a nursing admissions manager and lives in a close-knit community in Richmond, Virginia. She's the mother of two teenage boys and divides her time between work, church activities, and her family. Iesha is well known among her friends and in her community for her endless kindness, her laughter, her loyalty, and her incredible discipline.

Iesha is also someone for whom the impact of institutional retribution bias has been tremendous—her felony record for two separate nonviolent, non-drug-related crimes has permeated her life in social, spiritual, and financial ways far beyond the reasonable limits of her convictions. In the early 2000s, Iesha deposited four bad checks at an ATM during a time when she was struggling to make ends meet. Because there were four separate checks, and because she deposited them at an ATM, Iesha was charged with nine separate felony charges and her life was radically altered when she served three years for these charges, handing over her newborn infant son when she was first locked up. She describes how having a felony record takes much of her emotional energy, even years after being released:

I think about [my record] every time I think about new opportunities, whether it be careerwise, if I want to volunteer at my kids' school, any opportunity that I know for a fact would consider my background makes me think about it, and I quickly eliminate the possibility if the opportunity could even be for me because I have a background. I have come to believe that no matter the reason for my background, because I have a background, I'm immediately going to be shot down, so I won't even try for new things.

You can take the promotion at my job that I recently got—I didn't apply for it, they had to seek me

out. I wouldn't have applied for it because of my back-
ground. I was working as a receptionist initially. She
thought I had a great personality and was warm and
welcoming, and she told me she thought I'd be a great
fit for this new role.

But I often wonder if she knows about my back-
ground, if she's actually reviewed the files. I wonder if
my job performance will be enough to keep my job? I've
heard that they run background checks every year
and I often get concerned if my background has been
seen. I have this low-level anxiety all the time. I have
just decided that I just have to do the best that I
have and hope and pray that my performance will
just speak for myself.

Iesha's workplace anxiety is about more than just a desire to be employed and provide for her family. And countless studies show that living with even low levels of stress and anxiety can wreak havoc on a person's physiological wellbeing. Iesha must keep a steady income in order to continue paying the courts for her felony charges. Each month for the past 15 years, she has paid three separate Virginia courts 10 percent of her total monthly income, which is no small feat for a single mother of two teenage boys. Her payments are for court costs and felony fines and if she misses a payment, Iesha will forfeit her driver's license. If she forfeits her license, she will be unable to get to her job which, in part, enables her to pay her fines.

At her current rate, Iesha estimates that she will pay the courts off in ten years. Should she lose her license, she will be unable to take her boys to school or get to and from the places that she needs to get to in order to maintain the life that she has worked so hard to put back together. While she was still on probation immediately following her release, missing this payment would have meant reincarceration for Iesha, so keeping up with this payment has, at times, meant not paying other bills in order to keep this bill paid above all else.

> *To be honest, even now, financially, short of Jesus, I would not make it. It's impossible the way the system is set up. I don't know if this is intentionally that way but after being incarcerated, I cannot make ends meet. I am on salary, but I work 50 to 60 hours a week because I feel pressure to overperform because I want to be so good that if they ever see my record they'll have my performance and my presence to look at.*
>
> *Because the cards are stacked against me, I cannot give less than 200 percent. That means my job controls my life. That means my kids, my friends, nothing else gets my time but my job—that's just my reality. This is what it means in order for me to sustain my life.*

Though her physical incarceration is over, Iesha says, "this punishment that was supposed to be three years is essentially a lifetime." Iesha's "crime" has exacted far more than a proportionate penalty, demanding that she literally pay hundreds of times over the original cost of her crime and robbed her of years with her boys. Iesha has fought to have her right to vote restored, and has begun to share her story with others outside of her community in Richmond.

Retribution Bias and Employment

One of the biggest challenges for Iesha, and for others like her, is the difficulty that comes with getting a job after a felony conviction. Employment presents a significant challenge for folks coming out of incarceration. Though many employers come to the realization that even folks with the most serious felonies can make great employees, as is backed up by multiple studies,[1] as many as three out of four people remain unemployed a year after release from prison, and just 12.5 percent of employers say they will accept job applications from an ex-offender because they think doing so would impact their business.[2] Many people raise the issue of background checks as a metric for determining who they should hire and Iesha's experience demonstrates how heavily the background check looms over the heads of those who have felony convictions on their records.

Iesha's story demonstrates again the power of getting close and learning the stories of people who have been impacted by the criminal justice system and retribution bias. Her workplace performance has been noticed by her colleagues and she has managed to earn a promotion.

The felony challenge, however, is a largely a perceptual one that is rooted in our retribution bias. The problem is not that ex-offenders are somehow bad employees or that it would be too risky to employee them. Northwestern's Workplace Science Project has researched the question of how it actually impacts business's bottom line to hire people with criminal records and Deborah Weiss, the study's lead researcher and director, has concluded that people who look to background checks to determine a potential hire's risk to the company are "overreacting."[3] She says there is occasionally a very slightly elevated misconduct risk. When quantified, it does not amount to money saved; people hired with records often stay with companies longer. Furthermore, it does not take into account that criminal records are distributed unevenly, given to those who are poor more often than to those who have the financial resources to build a good legal defense. Their conclusion? You should always be diligent about who you hire. Criminal justice records are, by and large, not good indicators of who is a riskier hire.[4]

Oftentimes, retribution bias is masked in hiring policies that make it difficult to employ undocumented people, criminalizing employers who hire them. Our friend Lana Heath de Martinez works in public policy doing advocacy for immigration issues, and as a white woman she has worked hard to continually evaluate her role in institutional bias and elevate the voices of those who are most impacted by unjust immigration policies. She shared a time with us when consequences of retribution bias had a direct impact on her work:

> *I am constantly thinking that I should not be the person doing this job. At least, it should not be just me. So, during the summer when I had the opportunity to hire a year-long fellow, I prioritized finding someone from the impacted community. Two women quickly became outstanding candidates, both from Mexico, both with uncertain immigration status.*
>
> *I was so excited to put my money (well, the organization's) where my mouth is and invest in leadership from the impacted community. But I couldn't hire either woman. The fellowship is funded by a denomination that stipulated the person be hired as a full-time employee with benefits. Without a social security number, my two best candidates were not options. I hired an excellent fellow who shares my commitment to intersectionality and deference to those most impacted by policy, but yet again, the money, benefits, and opportunities are withheld from those we say we should follow. I guess their leadership is expected to be free.*

American criminalization of the other has historically set up systems that ostracize and subdue minority people for the gain of those in power. The means to work are withheld or hidden behind absurdly complex systems as a form of punishment for those who have entered our country's borders. Even as Lana has worked to bring light to these issues, she herself has found herself facing the same systems at play that she works to fight to end. Lana writes that:

> *Every day is an ethical quandary for me. I use every opportunity to amplify and elevate the voices and experiences of people who are undocumented. And I am getting paid to do that work while the people I seek to amplify and elevate are usually not compensated.*
>
> *I love my job, but I also really deeply love the communities I work with and I hate benefiting from a system that contributes to their oppression. Instead of saying, "We can't hire you because you don't have a social security number" why aren't we saying, "How can we create a place for you here?"*

For the communities that Lana works to advocate on behalf of, retribution bias says that these communities deserve punishment and denial through racial stereotyping and criminal language. But in addition to their contributions of humanity, gifts, and abilities, immigrants are actually a net positive for the American economy and make important contributions across the workforce.[5]

Martha Rollins, a local antique dealer in Richmond, experienced this firsthand when she was running her shop and regularly moving furniture. In the late 1990s, Martha became aware that while there were wealthy white customers coming in the front of her shop, the people helping to move the furniture in the back of her shop were mostly African American men in their late

20s to early 40s, and most lacked full-time employment. After knowing many of them for some time, eating lunch with them, and developing friendships with many of them, Martha became curious about why they were unable to secure full-time employment. They all expressed a desire for full-time employment and, from her vantage point, were kind, intelligent, creative, and smart people. So, she finally asked one day, and they shared with her that they'd all been incarcerated and their felony backgrounds made full-time employment virtually unattainable. "It made me notice," shared Martha.

Gradually, over time, Martha became involved with the prison system and the more involved she became, the more she described her understanding of the prison system to be like the primary antagonist of *Les Miserables*, Javert. A police officer, Javert is obsessed with retribution and pursues Jean Valjean throughout the story for his crime. Javert eventually drowns himself in the river Seine when he cannot reconcile his ethical system with the idea that Jean Valjean is more than his transgression.

In hopes of creating a place where others could be seen as more than their transgressions, Martha worked with neighbors and community members to build Boaz and Ruth, a nonprofit focused on providing support, job training, and transitional support to folks coming out of the criminal justice system. Boaz and Ruth has grown to house several business ventures and a year-long job training program for people just coming out of the prison system.

Let's see how Martha has been doing the work of erasing institutional bias by looking at our six steps:

1. Set a clear intention.

Martha wanted to bridge the employment gap for her friends who she saw as gifted people whose presence was needed in the world and, yet, were struggling to find work because of a felony conviction.

2. Lead with data.

Martha's data came from learning more from neighbors in the economically depressed neighborhood where she lived, and from friends who shared stories of their own experiences with the prison system. It became clear that employment was a significant barrier to successful reentry for these people. Her prayer partner had been in a director role in the New York State Prison System and she participated in several round-table groups where those who had both worked with incarcerated people and had been incarcerated themselves were participants.

3. Diagnose accurately.

As Martha enlisted partners from her community to support her vision of empowering those who were coming out of the criminal justice system, the need she identified in those conversations with the men who she met at her antique shop was confirmed. Employment after a felony conviction was both a dire need and extremely difficult to obtain.

4. Deconstruct: eliminate subjective processes.

Martha's initial experience with this work issue revealed her own subjective biases: she assumed that good, smart people who were capable and wanted to work would always be able to get a job. As someone whose experiences were quite different from those who were returning from incarceration, she felt it important to eliminate subjective processes by refusing to lead the initiative alone.

5. Reconstruct with objectivity.

Martha reconstructed her jobs initiative and shared leadership with Rosa Jiggets, a woman who had deep roots in Highland Parks and expressed a desire to work with Martha on the transitional jobs for ex-offenders. This helped Boaz and Ruth's be a more objectively welcoming space.

6. Build accountability and ongoing measurement.

While Boaz and Ruth's measures of success were less about numbers and more about lives that were transformed, their accountability was primarily set toward the community in which they were housed. Thus, while there were people from outside of the community on the board and serving as volunteers, Martha and other staff have worked diligently to always protect the places of community leadership.

Another way they have stayed accountable to their intention includes a commitment to changing the language used about people who have come into contact with the criminal justice system. They have done this is by framing re-entry in terms of one of their core principles, "The release of a prisoner is a release of tremendous gifts and abilities (as well as potential earning power and tax revenue) into communities in great need of those gifts."[6] This language directly confronts images of criminality and invites both ex-offenders and communities to rebuild with an air of hope and optimism.

Retribution Bias and Business

Martha and Boaz and Ruth have been working to erase institutional bias by supporting ex-offenders themselves. Still others work to erase institutional bias by confronting the policies and procedures that are in place that contribute to the incarceration epidemic. While it may seem difficult to conceptualize what a for-profit business could do to confront retribution bias, business and corporate voices carry significant policy weight. Another friend (and Ashley's husband), Alex Mejias, is the president of the Business Coalition for Justice, which was formed out of Alex's own experiences with retribution bias and his conversations as a business leader and community member. Alex writes:

> *Throughout 2015 and 2016, as police killings of inno-cent and unarmed men of color seemed to proliferate on social media, my boss and I began to have conver-sations about what, if anything, we could do as a busi-ness to affect change. We saw the toll that these incidents were taking on our African American team members and read about the potential days of protest.*
>
> *Everything seemed to be happening at the individ-ual level, but it seemed like perhaps we could partici-pate as a business and leverage the added influence we had as a business. Things came to a head for me on September 16, 2016, when I watched Terence Crutcher die with his hands in the air, unarmed and innocent. I couldn't sleep that night. I was angry, but also scared to my core.*
>
> *A few years back, I had been threatened by a police officer in Charlottesville, Virginia, who told me that not pulling out my registration fast enough was "a good way to get my teeth knocked in." Upon moving to Richmond, Virginia, I once was pulled over twice in the same night by Henrico County Police after borrow-ing a white friend's car with expired tags (he had never been pulled over).*

*But that night it became clear, in a visceral way,
that my life was at risk. But beyond myself, I thought
about all of the victims of police brutality going back
generations and felt powerless against this seemingly
institutionalized and engrained ritual.*

Alex approached his boss and asked if he was serious about actually doing something. When his boss said yes, they got to work brainstorming ways to think about these issues and to be proactive.

*We first imagined a day of protest, when we and other
like-minded businesses would close our doors to protest police brutality. We pitched the idea to our
upstairs neighbors at TMI Consulting and they were
immediately on board. As a tech company, we reached
out to some other shops and found a few more willing
businesses. But some businesses were hesitant and we
knew we'd need to explain ourselves. So I decided to
draft a statement explaining our rationale and goals.*

*We began circulating the letter and asking other
businesses to sign on. As more and more businesses got
involved, we heard the desire for conversation,
amongst businesses and even with the police. Moving
organically, we decided to shift from a day of protest
to a moment of conversation, when we as the local
business community could gather with the police to
talk about the issue of police brutality and how we
could prevent it from happening in our hometown.*

*We called it Businesses for Black Lives (#B4BL).
That meeting happened, coincidentally, the day after*

Donald Trump was elected. In a way, that reality put us all on edge, but also gave many of us a new resolve to actually work harder, knowing that the local government would now need to shoulder much more of the heavy work of dismantling structural racism. After #B4BL, many of us wanted to continue meeting and finding ways to work together to undo institutional racism.

Alex developed a steering committee with a few other business leaders and together they decided on a mission, vision, and name for the organization. They gathered input through surveys and got an overwhelming response that businesses wanted to be organized together to face these issues, so in May of 2017, they incorporated as the Business Coalition for Justice (BCJ).

Starting slowly, we decided upon two projects: first, a letter to the Virginia House of Delegates Subcommittee on Criminal Law regarding the felony larceny dollar threshold which, at $200, had not been updated in nearly 40 years. Second, we decided to help birth a charitable bail fund for the Richmond area, which is now called the Richmond Community Bail Fund.

Along with these initiatives, we plan to provide resources and support to businesses who join the BCJ, helping them seek racial equity within their businesses. We encourage all of our members to seek racial equity in four areas: hiring and diversity, company culture, supply chain, and community engagement.

Here is Alex and the Business Coalition for Justice's work against retribution bias.

1. **Set a clear intention.**

   Alex wanted to find a way, as a business, to leverage his workplace's influence to work against the criminalization of minority people.

2. **Lead with data.**

   Alex and his coworkers brainstormed ideas and then gathered the data they needed to see if their idea (a day of protest) would be effective by circulating a letter describing their intent to other businesses in the community.

3. **Diagnose accurately.**

   As they circulated this letter, they were able to determine that while the issue of criminalization of minority people was on everyone's mind, the business community had a strong desire for conversation amongst businesses and even with local police and specifically surrounding the issue of the felony dollar threshold. This gave the leadership of the BCJ a clear path forward.

4. **Deconstruct: eliminate subjective processes.**

   Like Tim Ryan at PwC, Alex and the BCJ disrupted the status quo by making space for conversation between police and business owners who wanted to voice their concerns.

5. **Reconstruct with objectivity.**

   Alex and the BCJ began to create a new objective space by making room for conversation between business leaders with concerns and local police.

6. Build accountability and ongoing measurement.

Alex and the BCJ established four areas of measurement for racial equity that coalition members are committed to. The BCJ has also taken up the cause of advocating for a specific policy measure, the felony larceny threshold.

While retribution bias can seem overwhelming to tackle, each of these folks began with their own experience and understanding of what it means to encounter another human being. The strength and sting of retribution bias will only stand as long as you allow the myth of criminalization to say that another person can be measured and understood by what she or he has done in her life. And often times, when we reach back into our own stories, we begin to realize that the marks of the justice system aren't given equally. But that realization can bring us to a place of compassion and strengthen our fight for equity for others.

Conclusion

Where to Start Your Organizational Journey of Erasing Institutional Bias

Institutional bias is as pervasive as any individual, interpersonal bias. Humans are inherently biased. And as long as people are building systems, those institutions will be vulnerable to the liability that is human bias. The phenomenon itself is not insurmountable. All we need are people like you who are willing to stand up and demand change in the face of institutional bias.

Using the six steps outlined in this book, any individual has the tools and the power to erase institutional biases one-by-one. From gender bias to retribution bias, we each have the power and responsibility to own the parts we have played in perpetuating bias and to redefine our roles in restoring systemic balance.

Whether you see yourself as a leader at your organization or just a regular person, this work starts where you are. Take the time to look at the system in which you are embedded. Be realistic about the scope of influence you have and please don't skip the Preliminary Personal Work. CEOs and individual contributors must ask themselves the hard questions before embarking on this journey. Once you have done that, then you can review the organizational perspective and follow the six steps for erasing institutional bias.

This is not a solo journey, so find allies, cultivate them carefully, and work as a team to expand your limited personal view of what is happening at your workplace. Even senior executives can't see everything that is taking place at work. In fact, leaders have a distinctly distorted view that often contributes to sustaining institutional bias. Why? Because people are not always brave enough to tell leaders what they need to know. But leaders do need to know. So whether you are the leader aiming to purge systemic bias from your organization, or the regular person who will ultimately deliver a well-researched, data-backed, thoroughly vetted and supported report to leadership, you've got your work cut out for you.

As you do the work, you may be left with a sense of guilt—white guilt, male guilt, institutional guilt—you get the idea. That sense of shame is linked to internalized culpability. This is where we have to remind you that bias itself is not your fault. Bias is a function of your imperfect human brain—a complex organ hardwired for survival. If you are white, you did not create racism, so let it go. Don't let go of the sense of personal responsibility entirely, just the self-deprecating aspect. You didn't create racism but you do have a responsibility to address it where you stand.

If you are male, you did not create sexism. It may have benefitted you and you may have engaged in less-than-ideal behavior toward people of other genders. So raise your awareness about your own actions and their impact on real humans and do better when you get the opportunity to make new choices. Wallowing in self-pity really doesn't help anyone. Turning toward right action can, though. Choose right action next time. There is always a next time.

And if you are part of an organization that takes on the really hard work of erasing institutional bias, you may dig around in your company's history and learn some really frightening stuff. Your group may have shameful things to make amends for, from supporting slavery while it was still legal to deliberately underpaying women and otherwise discriminating against sexual and gender minorities. If you find the filthy underbelly, resist the urge to bury it. That only makes things worse. Tell the truth about what's been done and to whom. Then make efforts to reconcile with authentic consideration for those affected. Shame exists in the shadows. This work isn't sexy, but it's necessary. The truth will set you (and your organization) free.

Each of the systemic biases we enumerated in this book has its own inherent challenges and implications. While we do not encourage people or institutions to compare struggles, retribution bias has one of the most devastating individual and collective impacts among the institutional biases covered in this book. One reason is because retribution bias intersects with racial and socio-economic bias to create devastating results.

If you take a closer look at the communities around you, you will encounter people affected by many of the systemic biases in this book. But the number of people and the severity of the impact of institutional bias will increase exponentially as the communities you engage with are more marginalized and less affluent. If you are in the United States, that means browner and poorer. In other countries, populations may be marginalized by religion, gender, or some other variable.

Regardless of country, societies find ways to marginalize groups of people and embed bias into systems to keep them disadvantaged and oppressed. These disparate consequences must be addressed, and we cannot wait for someone else to fix them. It is up to each of us to take up a cause we can connect with and make change happen where we live and work. Whether you are a seasoned change-maker or you are brand new to the struggle, we welcome you to our ranks, and we thank you for your commitment to making the world a more diverse, inclusive, and equitable place.

Notes

Introduction

1. L. R. James, "A Conditional Reasoning Measure for Aggression," *Organizational Research Methods*, vol 8, (2005): 69–99.

Chapter 1

1. Ruy Teixeira and John Halpin, "Building an All-In Nation," Center for American Progress, October 22, 2013, https://www.americanprogress.org/issues/race/reports/2013/10/22/77665/building-an-all-in-nation, accessed December 11, 2017.

2. Caryn Block, Sandy Koch, Benjamin Liberman, Tarani Merriwether, and Loriann Merriwether, "Contending with Stereotype Threat at Work: A Model of Long-Term Responses." *The Counseling Psychologist*, 39, no. 4 (2011): 571. https://www.apa.org/education/ce/stereotype-threat.pdf, accessed December 4, 2017.

Chapter 4

1. Melanie Tannenbaum, "The Problem When Sexism Just Sounds So Darn Friendly . . ." *PsySociety* (blog) *Scientific American*, April 2, 2013, https://blogs.scientificamerican.com/psysociety/benevolent-sexism.

2. Tannebaum.

3. Amy Davidson Sorkin, "Yvonne Brill and the Beef-Stroganoff Illusion," *The New Yorker*, April 1, 2013. https://www.nytimes .com/2013/03/31/science/space/yvonne-brill-rocket-scientist -dies-at-88.html

4. Peter Glick and Susan Fiske, "BS at Work: How Benevolent Sexism Undermines Women and Justifies Backlash" (Harvard Business School Research Symposium: Gender and Work, 2013)

5. Tannebaum.

6. Glick.

7. Glick.

8. Glick.

Chapter 5

1. Greg Howard, "The Easiest Way to Get Rid of Racism? Just Redefine It." *New York Times*, August 16, 2016, www.nytimes .com/2016/08/21/magazine/the-easiest-way-to-get-rid-of -racism-just-redefine-it.html, accessed December 4, 2017.

2. "Criminal Justice Fact Sheet." NAACP, www.naacp.org /criminal-justice-fact-sheet, accessed December 4, 2017.

3. "Criminal Justice Fact Sheet." NAACP.

4. Jack Zenger and Joseph Folkman, "Leaders Aren't Great at Judging How Inclusive They Are," *Harvard Business Review*, October 26, 2017, hbr.org/2017/10/leaders-arent-great-at -judging-how-inclusive-they-are, accessed December 22, 2017).

5. James Surowiecki, "The Widening Racial Wealth Divide," *The New Yorker*, https://www.newyorker.com/magazine/2016 /10/10/the-widening-racial-wealth-divide.

6. Sylvia Ann Hewlett, Melinda Marshall, and Trudy Bourgeois, "People Suffer at Work When They Can't Discuss the Racial Bias They Face Outside of It," *Harvard Business Review*, https://hbr.org/2017/07/people-suffer-at-work-whe-they -cant-discuss-the-racial-bias-they-face-outside-of-it.

7. Hewlett, Marshall, and Bourgeois, "People Suffer at Work When They Can't Discuss the Racial Bias They Face Outside of It."

8. Rae Ellen Bichell, "Scientists Start to Tease Out the Subtler Ways Racism Hurts Health," NPR, November 11, 2017, www.npr.org/sections/health-shots/2017/11/11/562623815 /scientists-start-to-tease-out-the-subtler-ways-racism-hurts -health, accessed December 28, 2017.

9. Bichell.

10. Bichell.

11. Adapted from Kenney, G. (2014). *Interrupting Microaggressions*, College of the Holy Cross, Diversity Leadership & Education. Accessed on-line at https://www .holycross.edu/sites/default/files/files/centerforteaching /interrupting_microaggressions_january2014.pdf, October 2014.

12. Ella B. Smith, Sylvia Ann Hewlett, Trevor Phillips, and Ripa Rashad, "Easing Racial Tensions at Work," Center for Talent Innovation, 2017. http://www.talentinnovation.org /publication.cfm?publication=1570, accessed March 08, 2018.

13. Maxine Williams, "Numbers Only Take Us So Far," *Harvard Business Review*, October 24, 2017, hbr.org/2017/11/numbers -take-us-only-so-far, accessed December 28, 2017.

14. Williams.

15. Williams.

16. Williams.

17. Tim Ryan, "'The Silence was Deafening'—Why We need to Talk about Race," LinkedIn (blog), July 22, 2016, https://www .linkedin.com/pulse/silence-deafening-why-we-need-talk-race -timothy-f-ryan?trk=prof-post, accessed December 31, 2017.

18. Emily Peck, "What Happened When One CEO Decided to Talk Openly About Race," *Huffington Post*, December 12, 2016, www.huffingtonpost.com/entry/workplace-diversity-pwc_us _584af4fbe4b0bd9c3dfc976b, accessed December 30, 2017.

19. Ellen McGirt, "Tim Ryan's Awakening," *Fortune*, February 1, 2017, fortune.com/pwc-diversity-tim-ryan, accessed December 27, 2017.

20. McGirt.

21. McGirt.

22. McGirt.

23. Carl Zimmer, "A Single Migration from Africa Populated the World, Studies Find," *New York Times*, September 21, 2016, www.nytimes.com/2016/09/22/science/ancient-dna-human -history.html, accessed January 16, 2018.

Chapter 6

1. Tiffany Jana and Matthew Freeman, *Overcoming Bias: Building Authentic Relationships across Differences* (Oakland, CA: Berrett-Koehler Publishers, 2016), 74.

2. Stefanie K. Johnson, David R. Hekman, and Elsa T. Chan, "If There's Only One Woman in Your Candidate Pool, There's Statistically No Chance She'll Be Hired," *Harvard Business Review*, April 26, 2016, https://hbr.org/2016/04/if-theres-only -one-woman-in-your-candidate-pool-theres-statistically-no -chance-shell-be-hired, accessed May 22, 2018.

3. Lincoln Quillian, Devah Pager, Ole Hexel, and Arnfinn H. Midtbøen, "The Persistence of Racial Discrimination in Hiring," *Proceedings of the National Academy of Sciences*, October 2017, 114, no. 41: 10870–10875. https://doi.org /10.1073/pnas.1706255114.

Chapter 7

1. Carolina Moreno and Riley Arthur. "25 Times White Actors Played People of Color and No One Really Gave a S**t." *Huffington Post*, February 23, 2017, www.huffingtonpost.com /entry/26-times-white-actors-played-people-of-color-and-no

-one-really-gave-a-sht_us_56cf57e2e4b0bf0dab313ffc, accessed January 10, 2018.

2. Darnell Hunt and Ana-Christina Ramón,"2015 Hollywood Diversity Report," Ralph J. Bunche Center for African American Studies, February 25, 2015, bunchecenter.ucla.edu /2015/02/25/2015-hollywood-diversity-report: 2–3, accessed January 10, 2018.

3. Alyin Zafa, "Physical Video Games May Help the Older Psychologically," *The Atlantic*, February 13, 2011, https://www.theatlantic.com/technology/archive/2011/02/ physical-video-games-may-help-the-elderly-psychologically /71184, accessed April 9, 2018.

4. Michael Lynn and Zachary Brewster, "What's Behind Racial Differences in Restaurant Tipping?" *The Washington Post*, January 21, 2015, www.washingtonpost.com/posteverything /wp/2015/01/21/whats-behind-racial-differences-in -restaurant-tipping, accessed January 8, 2018.

5. John Murden, "An Overview of Poverty, Race, and Jurisdiction in Metropolitan Richmond," *Church Hill People's News*, October 10, 2010, https://chpn.net/2010/10/06/an -overview-of-poverty-race-and-jurisdiction-in-metropolitan- richmond, accessed January 8, 2018

Chapter 8

1. "A Living Death: Life Without Parole for Nonviolent Offenses," American Civil Liberties Union Foundation, 2013, https://www.aclu.org/files/assets/111813-lwop-complete- report.pdf, accessed March 20, 2018.

2. Wendy Sawyer and Alex Clark, "New Data: The Rise of the Prosecutor Politician," Prison Policy Initiative, March 2017, https://www.prisonpolicy.org/blog/2017/07/13/prosecutors, accessed April 3, 2018.

3. Elliot Currie, *Crime and Punishment in America* (New York: Metropolitan Books, Henry Holt & Company, 1998), https://archive.nytimes.com/www.nytimes.com/books/first /c/currie-crime.html, accessed April 7, 2018.

4. Currie.

5. Nazgol Ghandnoosh, "Race and Punishment: Racial Perceptions of Crime and Support for Punitive Policies," The Sentencing Project, 2014, www.sentencingproject.org /publications/race-and-punishment-racial-perceptions-of-crime-and-support-for-punitive-policies, accessed January 4, 2018.

6. Ghandnoosh.

7. Ghandnoosh.

8. Ghandnoosh.

9. Roy Walmsley, *World Prison Population List,* tenth 2012 ed.: 1, prisonstudies.org/sites/default/files/resources/downloads /wppl_10.pdf, accessed January. 1, 2018.

10. Thomas Jefferson, *Notes on the State of Virgina,* Queries 14 and 18: 137–142, 162–163, http://press-pubs.uchicago.edu /founders/documents/v1ch15s28.html, accessed January 7, 2018.

11. Ashley Diaz Mejias, "The Illusion of Black and White," TMI Blog, https://www.tmiconsultinginc.com/illusion-black -white, accessed January 12, 2018.

12. Angela F. Chan, "America Never Abolished Slavery." *Huffington Post*, March 2, 2015, www.huffingtonpost.com /angela-f-chan/america-never-abolished-slavery_b_6777420 .html, accessed January 5, 2018.

13. "Black Codes and Pig Laws," Public Broadcasting Service, www.pbs.org/tpt/slavery-by-another-name/themes/black-codes, accessed January 9, 2018.

14. Sarah Childress, "Michelle Alexander: 'A System of Racial and Social Control.'" PBS, Public Broadcasting Service, April 29,

2014, www.pbs.org/wgbh/frontline/article/michelle-alexander
-a-system-of-racial-and-social-control/. (accessed Jan. 9, 2018)

15. Judge Frederic Block, "Racism's Hidden History in the War on
Drugs." *Huffington Post*, January 3, 2013, www.huffingtonpost
.com/judge-frederic-block/war-on-drugs_b_2384624.html,
accessed January 1, 2018.

16. Block.

17. Richard Pérez-Peña, "Contrary to Trump's Claims,
Immigrants Are Less Likely to Commit Crimes," *New York
Times*, January 26, 2017, www.nytimes.com/2017/01/26/us
/trump-illegal-immigrants-crime.html, accessed January 15,
2018.

18. Nazgol Ghandnoosh, "Race and Punishment: Racial
Perceptions of Crime and Support for Punitive Policies,"
The Sentencing Project, 2014, www.sentencingproject.org
/publications/race-and-punishment-racial-perceptions-of
-crime-and-support-for-punitive-policies, accessed January 4,
2018.

19. T. Bonczar, "Prevalence of Imprisonment in the U.S.
Population, 1974–2001," 2013, Washington, DC: Bureau of
Justice Statistics, http://www.sentencingproject.org/criminal
-justice-facts, accessed January 5, 2018.

20. Nazgol Ghandnoosh. "Race and Punishment: Racial
Perceptions of Crime and Support for Punitive Policies."

Chapter 9

1. Marina Duane et al., "Criminal Background Checks Impact
on Employment and Recidivism," The Urban Institute, March
2017, https://www.urban.org/research/publication/criminal-
background-checks-impact-employment-and-recidivism,
accessed April 23, 2018.

2. Brentin Mock, "Excluding Ex-Offenders from the Workforce
Is Bad Business." *CityLab*, June 15, 2017, www.citylab.com

/equity/2017/06/the-case-for-hiring-ex-offenders/529896, accessed January 1, 2018.

3. Mock.

4. Dylan Minor, Nicola Persico, and Deborah M. Weiss, "Criminal Background and Job Performance," Abstract. Northwestern University, Kellogg School of Management, May 11, 2017. papers.ssrn.com/sol3/papers.cfm?abstract_id =2851951, accessed January 16, 2018.

5. Marshall Fitz, "Immigrants Are Makers, Not Takers," Center for American Progress, December 19, 2013, www.americanprogress.org/issues/immigration/news/2013 /02/08/52377/immigrants-are-makers-not-takers, accessed January 14, 2018.

6. "Mission Strategies," on Boaz and Ruth's website, 2018, http://www.boazandruth.com/index.cfm/topic/missionstrat.

Acknowledgments

Tiffany Jana

I would like to acknowledge my God, first and foremost. Through Him all things are possible, including this book. To my coauthor, Ashley Mejias, for being a brave ocelot in the face of a big, daunting challenge. My parents, Gene and Deborah Egerton, for believing in me even in my moments of doubt. Mom, thanks for giving me a heart for the world by always showing me yours. My esteemed colleagues: especially the indomitable Laura Swanson Bowser for her endless patience with me and for running the show while I write books and start tech firms; the gentle spirit Kelley Wendt for seeing my vision and supporting my authorship; the genius force multiplier Milgo Yonis for unlocking the secrets of diversity and bias in technology; Skyler Broughman for forgiving me my foibles, researching institutional bias into the wee hours, and keeping me in stitches and on track; my beautiful Time Lord Dylan Jones for time-traveling with my youngest and making space for me to get this book to the people; and Travis Clark for stopping time with blessed musical instruction so Saba wouldn't miss her mama so much while she was writing. Also, the fabulous Berrett-Koehler Publishing team has been an absolute dream to work with on this book as well as my first book, *Overcoming Bias*. Thank you to my mentors Kelly Chopus and Christy Coleman for your faithfulness and for never allowing me to let the tsunamis of life sink me. And my BFFs Ebony Green, Lisa Speller, Bunny Young, and Dawit Worku for listening to me whine on my worst days and celebrating with me on my best days.

I also want to acknowledge the growing team of American Truth and Reconciliation founders for further fueling the fire of my passion for social justice: Jay Coen Gilbert, Nike Irvin, Kevin Eppler, Michael Allen, Margot Brandenburg, Justin Wright, Carrie Norton, Gisele Shorter, Sharon Graci, John C. Few, Andrew Henderson, and Ann Marie Stieritz.

Finally, I dedicate this book to my eldest daughter, Naomi. At the writing of this book, Naomi was a Harvard freshman and already making friends and making her mark. Dedicated to social justice causes since she was old enough to understand that all people were created equal but not treated as such, Naomi consistently chose right action from the earliest age. She's a trustworthy friend, a devoted daughter and granddaughter, a loving sister, a dedicated student, an upright mentor, and a brilliant woman. Her heart beats for the world. Being her mother has been one of the greatest joys of my life. It brings me great pride and peace to know that when I am no longer, the company and legacy I have spent my life building will be left in her very capable hands. May God bless you always, my angel.

Ashley Diaz Mejias

Goodness, thank you to Alex Mejias. Joan Didion writes, "Our favorite people and our favorite stories become so not by any inherent virtue, but because they illustrate something deep in the grain, something unadmitted." You are my favorite person. You illustrate deep in the grain, the unadmitted, that the challenge and risk are worth it. Thank you for loving me. I love you. Thank you for all the extra you gave so that this could be real. Belen, Maisy, and Yves: you all make me more myself as you each become more of yourselves. And you each gave me courage to do something I didn't know I could do. Today, it's this book. I'm unspeakably proud to be yours and look forward with joy to seeing each of you make more of the things that bring light into the world. Also, thank you to my coauthor, Tiffany Jana—thank you for believing in me and thank you for being the kind of woman who brings others alongside her as she rises. You inspire me and you have taught me what it means to silence the voices that say "You cannot!" and to soar. I'm still pretty amazed I get to be your friend. Thank you, Skyler, for your unending work, your endless patience, and sharing your brilliance with this book—you made this happen. And thank you, Berrett-Koehler Publishing team, for walking a new writer through the process and for taking a risk on an unknown from Richmond. My parents, Nelson and Beth Diaz, for being both the firmest foundations and the most reassuring launch pads.

And finally, my friends. I have a cloud of witnesses, the deepest friends for whom the work of moving against the specters of bias in the world is as deep in their bones, is the marrow of life. Thank you for sharing your stories with me, for risking. And more, thank you each: Sara Miller, Grace, my Rhodes friends, my RVA community for each text and prayer, for each "how's the book going?", for your own journeys of strength and challenging bias in the world. I could never write another word and live with great hope for the world knowing the way that you all do life, do friendships, do parenting, do love.

Index

About the Authors

Tiffany Jana

Tiffany Jana found her way to this book by way of her first book, *Overcoming Bias*. She is the CEO of a global network of socially responsible, interconnected companies that cultivate organizational inclusion around the world. She has spent two decades following in her mother's footsteps and coloring outside the lines along the way. Her Army Brat upbringing, and subsequent infatuation with travel, exposed Dr. Jana to dozens of countries and cultures that made her question whether all of the focus on difference and discrimination was the best use of human energy. Tiffany has always believed that if she could only help people see the vast depth, complexity, and beauty of the human experience, that perhaps people would be kinder to each other. So whether she was performing poetry on stage, painting on canvas, acting out the trials and tragedies of various theatrical characters, interviewing or being interviewed, writing journalistic human interest stories, or simply sharing her own experiences, it has always been about helping people see each other more fully and more clearly. "It's harder to hate when you know what people have been through. Our joys and our sadness may be attributable to different narratives, but the sensory experience of raw human emotion is the same regardless of your color, gender, race, religion, nationality, sexual orientation, or any other characteristic we use to divide ourselves."

Ashley Diaz Mejias

Photo by Milgo Yonis

Ashley Diaz Mejias is half Cuban and half Scotch-Irish, is married to a Haitian–Puerto Rican, and got here because she has always had a lot of folks around her asking hard questions. Including Tiffany, who asked "do you want to coauthor?" Originally from Memphis, Tennessee, Ashley began regularly challenging systemic bias while working as the educational director for a small nonprofit after graduating from college. Since then, she has spent too many years in graduate school, devoting her work to researching and writing about racial bias. Ashley has written for blogs and led curricula for institutional and congregational conversations on race, systemic bias, and mass incarceration and is currently a candidate for ordination in the Presbyterian Church, USA. When she's not wishing she was more organized or wiping goldfish crumbs from her eyes, she is working with an amazing group of folks to grow the Richmond Community Bail Fund and pastoring at the Lord Jesus Korean Presbyterian Church. She now lives with her husband and three young daughters in the East End of Richmond, Viriginia. This is her first book.

About TMI Consulting

TMI Consulting was founded in 2010 as a diversity and inclusion management consulting company. In 2012, the partnership merged with a diversity Benefit Corporation and a marketing LLC founded in 2003. TMI Consulting, Inc. was the first diversity focused B Corporation in the world and earned national and international recognition in the field of organizational development and civic engagement. Today, TMI Consulting continues to provide diversity and inclusion consulting services and works in partnership with the rest of the TMI Portfolio companies to provide a range of socially responsible, interconnected organizations working to advance cultural inclusivity.

TMI Consulting supports organizations of all sizes, locally, nationally and internationally in a variety of capacities. Our work is industry and sector agnostic. We work with for-profit corporations, nonprofits, churches, universities, both foreign and domestic governments, and nongovernmental organizations.

Culture Focused Organizational Development

We help organizations build cohesive, accountable, diverse, inclusive, and equitable workplaces. We offer a full suite of diversity and inclusion services, ranging from full service organization-wide assessment and strategic planning, to keynotes and employee training.

Our keynote and training topics include Diversity, Equity, and Inclusion, Overcoming Unconscious Bias, Erasing Institutional Bias, Anti-Harassment, and Anti-Discrimination, The Ethics of

#MeToo in the Workplace, Social Entrepreneurship, Women in Leadership, and many more.

Our team uses innovative technologies to engage audiences in dynamic assessments, training, team and community meetings, and seminars. Our curricula can be tailored to meet the needs of each client.

What We Stand For

As a culture-focused organizational development consulting firm, we support organizations and communities across the United States and all over the world with some of their most challenging work. We are a values-driven company. Quality and integrity are critical to our business and we work hard to ensure that we deliver the highest level of service to all our clients.

Social Entrepreneurship and B Corp Status

As a certified B corporation, we have an ethical and legal commitment to providing a benefit to society. We measure our triple bottom-line (profit, people, planet) global impact using B Lab's B Impact Assessment. We've been named Best for the World (a two-year designation) in 2016 and 2018 for our global efficacy.

Also by Tiffany Jana and Matthew Freeman

Overcoming Bias
Building Authentic Relationships across Differences

Everybody's biased. The truth is, we all harbor unconscious assumptions that can get in the way of our good intentions and keep us from building authentic relationships with people different from ourselves. Tiffany Jana and Matthew Freeman use vivid stories and fun (yes, fun!) exercises and activities to help us reflect on our personal experiences and uncover how our hidden biases are formed. By becoming more self-aware, we can control knee-jerk reactions, conquer fears of the unknown, and prevail over closed-mindedness. In the end, Jana and Freeman's central message is that you are not the problem—but you can be the solution.

Paperback, 184 pages, ISBN 978-1-62656-725-2
PDF ebook, ISBN 978-1-62656-726-9
ePub ebook ISBN 978-1-62656-727-6
Digital Audio ISBN 978-1-62656-729-0

Berrett–Koehler Publishers, Inc.
www.bkconnection.com

800.929.2929

Berrett–Koehler
Publishers

Berrett-Koehler is an independent publisher dedicated to an ambitious mission: *Connecting people and ideas to create a world that works for all.*

We believe that the solutions to the world's problems will come from all of us, working at all levels: in our organizations, in our society, and in our own lives. Our BK Business books help people make their organizations more humane, democratic, diverse, and effective (we don't think there's any contradiction there). Our BK Currents books offer pathways to creating a more just, equitable, and sustainable society. Our BK Life books help people create positive change in their lives and align their personal practices with their aspirations for a better world.

All of our books are designed to bring people seeking positive change together around the ideas that empower them to see and shape the world in a new way.

And we strive to practice what we preach. At the core of our approach is Stewardship, a deep sense of responsibility to administer the company for the benefit of all of our stakeholder groups including authors, customers, employees, investors, service providers, and the communities and environment around us. Everything we do is built around this and our other key values of quality, partnership, inclusion, and sustainability.

This is why we are both a B-Corporation and a California Benefit Corporation—a certification and a for-profit legal status that require us to adhere to the highest standards for corporate, social, and environmental performance.

We are grateful to our readers, authors, and other friends of the company who consider themselves to be part of the BK Community. We hope that you, too, will join us in our mission.

A BK Business Book

We hope you enjoy this BK Business book. BK Business books pioneer new leadership and management practices and socially responsible approaches to business. They are designed to provide you with groundbreaking and practical tools to transform your work and organizations while upholding the triple bottom line of people, planet, and profits. High-five!

To find out more, visit **www.bkconnection.com.**

Berrett–Koehler
Publishers

Connecting people and ideas
to create a world that works for all

Dear Reader,

Thank you for picking up this book and joining our worldwide community of Berrett-Koehler readers. We share ideas that bring positive change into people's lives, organizations, and society.

To welcome you, we'd like to offer you a free e-book. You can pick from among twelve of our bestselling books by entering the promotional code **BKP92E** here: http://www.bkconnection.com/welcome.

When you claim your free e-book, we'll also send you a copy of our e-newsletter, the *BK Communiqué*. Although you're free to unsubscribe, there are many benefits to sticking around. In every issue of our newsletter you'll find

- A free e-book
- Tips from famous authors
- Discounts on spotlight titles
- Hilarious insider publishing news
- A chance to win a prize for answering a riddle

Best of all, our readers tell us, "Your newsletter is the only one I actually read." So claim your gift today, and please stay in touch!

Sincerely,

Charlotte Ashlock
Steward of the BK Website

Questions? Comments? Contact me at bkcommunity@bkpub.com.

MIX
Paper from
responsible sources
FSC® C016245

Certified

Corporation
bcorporation.net